C000226060

Fun Class Activities for Teachers: Book 1

To Gun Mårtensson, with love.

Peter Watcyn-Jones

Pearson Education Limited
Edinburgh Gate
Harlow
Essex CM20 2JE

ISBN 0 582 42785 1

First published 2000
Copyright © Peter Watcyn-Jones 2000

Designed by Mackerel
Illustrations by Mark Davis
Printed in Spain by Mateu Cromo, S. A. Pinto (Madrid)

Published by Pearson Education Limited in association with Penguin Books Ltd, both companies being subsidiaries of Pearson plc.

CONTENTS

* E: elementary LI: lower intermediate I: intermediate A: advanced

INTRODUCTION

Since I started writing I have always tried to include in my books the occasional exercise based on humour in one form or another – especially in my *Test Your Vocabulary* series (also published by Penguin). As a result, over the years I have built up a large collection of jokes, humorous stories, and so on, which, up until now, I have largely used as 'light relief' during talks and workshops. But so many teachers came up to me afterwards asking whether the material I had shown them was available in book form, that it got me thinking that perhaps such a book full of humorous and fun activities could be a very useful resource book for teachers. Fortunately, Penguin agreed, so here at long last is the book so many teachers have asked me for.

Fun Class Activities for Teachers consists of two books which form part of Penguin's growing series of photocopiable resource books for teachers. Although there are two books, they are to be thought of rather as two parts of the same book – one that would otherwise have been too bulky and cumbersome to use on its own. For this reason, whether you start with Book 1 or Book 2 is quite immaterial since both books contain activities at all levels, from Elementary to Advanced.

Fun Class Activities for Teachers: Book 1 contains a selection of 65 activities, the majority of which are based on humour in various forms, especially jokes and humorous stories. Most of them are designed for pairwork, groupwork and, occasionally, whole class activities. Most of the activity types found in this book are not really new but by using jokes, etc. instead of the more traditional and 'serious' types of texts, it is hoped that learning will be more fun and more stimulating for students

The organisation of Fun Class Activities: Book 1

The activities in *Fun Class Activities for Teachers: Book 1* have been grouped according to activity type. The contents section gives details of level plus type of activity. In this book, the activity types are: ice-breaker activity, matching pairs activities, jigsaw reading activities, misprints, etc., text activities and miscellaneous activities. Part 1 of the book gives detailed teacher's notes for each activity while Part 2 contains the various cards, handouts etc. to be photocopied. Where a key is necessary, this is included in the Teacher's Notes.

Classroom organisation

Although class sizes vary considerably, the book assumes an average class size of 10 – 20 students. Where possible, the classroom should be physically rearranged to facilitate working in pairs or groups.

However, should this not be possible, even the more traditional front-facing rows of desks can be easily adapted for pairwork and groupwork. For pairwork, students can either work with the person sitting next to them or the person in front of or behind them. For groupwork, two students can easily turn their chairs round to face two others behind them. Where you have an uneven number of students in the class, most pairwork activities can be done by three people (if necessary, two students against one).

The role of the teacher

For the majority of these games and activities the teacher's role is largely a passive one. The teacher is mainly responsible for:

- preparing the material in sufficient quantities

- explaining clearly what is to be done

- checking answers at the end of an activity

Once an activity has started, students work independently of the teacher at their own pace. The teacher goes round the classroom, listening and monitoring progress and only helping if absolutely necessary.

Time-limits

Most of the activities can be done in 15 – 20 minutes. For those odd occasions where it may be possible for an activity to go on and on, it is advisable to set a time-limit and to stop students whether they have finished or not. Apart from the obvious difficulties of students finishing at different times, the checking process is often an integral and, from the learning point of view, important part of the activity. As such, it is better that you check with the whole class rather than with individual groups.

Storing the material

The material to be photocopied can be divided into two types: **a** handouts which the students write on and **b** material which the students use but do not write on.

To save unnecessary work, therefore, it is a good idea that material that can be re-used should be made as durable as possible. One way is to mount everything on thin card. (Many photocopiers nowadays allow the use of card.) These cards and handouts can then be stored in separate envelopes (clearly labelled on the outside), which can be handed back at the end of the activity.

All the activities presented in this book require preparation on the part of the teacher. It is hoped that all the extra effort will prove to be rewarding.

PART 1 TEACHER'S NOTES
Ice-breaker activity

1   Have you heard the one about ...?   *Intermediate*

This activity is based on students telling each other jokes. It can be done by groups of up to 20 students.

Method

1. Copy and cut out the joke cards on page 16. Give each student a card.

2. The students work alone. Allow them time to read through and practise saying (quietly) their jokes.

3. Students now walk around the room telling their joke to up to eight different people. The people write down their name, then after hearing the joke, give it a mark out of 10.
   If necessary, you can write this opening prompt on the board:

   Hello, my name's ... Can I tell you a joke?

4. After a while, stop the activity, irrespective of whether everyone has spoken to eight people.

5. As a follow up, ask one or two students to look at their mark sheet and tell you which student's joke they found funniest.

Matching pairs activities

The activities in this section involve matching pairs of sentences. A lot of the activities here involve the use of jokes, puns or strange definitions.

2   Two-line jokes 1   *Elementary*

This is an activity based on two-line jokes, most of which are of a question and answer format. The students have to match a question with an appropriate answer.

Method

1. Copy and cut up the handouts on pages 18–19 – one set per pair.

2. Students work in pairs. Explain that they have to sort out twenty jokes. The first part of the joke is usually a question and is in bold type. Tell them to lay the cards out on the table or desk in front of them, with the first part of the joke on the left. Students then match these with the second part of the jokes.

3. Set a time-limit and check orally with the whole class by getting one pair to read out the first part of the joke and another pair to suggest the 'correct' response.

Key

The jokes on pages 18–27 are laid out in the correct order to make it easy to check.

3   Two-line jokes 2   *Intermediate*

Method

As Activity 2. The handouts are on page 20–21.

4   Two-line jokes 3   *Advanced*

Method

As Activity 2. The handouts are on pages 22–23.

5   Because ...1   *Elementary*

This is similar to the previous activity but this time it is based on questions starting with the word 'Why' and answers starting with the word 'Because ...'.

Method

As Activity 2. The handouts are on pages 24–25.

6   Because ... 2   *Intermediate*

Method

As Activity 2. The handouts are on pages 26–27.

7   'Daft' definitions   *Intermediate and above*

This is an activity based on matching words and definitions. But the definitions are not the expected ones!

Method

1. Students work individually or in pairs. Give each student/pair a copy of the handout on page 28.

2. Read through the introduction and the example. Allow 15–20 minutes for the students to work out their answers.

3. When everyone is ready, check the answers orally with the whole class.

Key

*0 g climate (climb it), 1 m optimist, 2 k life insurance,
3 f cannibal, 4 o smoker, 5 a accountant, 6 j gentleman,
7 e arrest (a rest), 8 b address (a dress), 9 l opera,
10 h commuter, 11 c adore (a door), 12 n school,
13 p tourist, 14 d afford (a Ford), 15 i dictionary
(in alphabetical order)*

8   Puns   *Advanced*

This is an activity based on puns. The students have to match up broken sentences.

Method

1. Students work individually or in pairs. Give each student/pair a copy of the handout on page 29.

2. Read through the introduction. Allow 15–20 minutes for the students to work out their answers.

3. Check the answers orally with the whole class.

1 e (football fan, fan for cold air), 2 m, 3 r, 4 i (A boomerang comes back when you throw it.), 5 t (Dalmatian dogs have distinctive black spots.), 6 p, 7 d, 8 n (sun days), 9 j, 10 f (A slip is a type of petticoat.), 11 a (a draw, a silk tie), 12 h, 13 q, 14 b, 15 k, 16 s, 17 c (hire = make higher), 18 g, 19 l (percussion instruments = drums, etc.), 20 o (You pluck a harp when you play it.)

---

9 'Chat up' lines   *Intermediate*

In this activity, students have to match up a question or statement with the correct (usually sarcastic) answer.

Method

1 Students work in pairs. Give each pair a copy of the handout on page 30.

2 Read through the introduction. Allow 10–15 minutes for the students to work out their answers.

3 When everyone is ready, check the answers orally with the whole class. Get one student to read out the man's line and another student to give the answer.

Key

1 d, 2 g, 3 j, 4 f, 5 a, 6 i, 7 b, 8 e, 9 h, 10 c

---

10 Who wrote what?   *Intermediate*

In this activity, students have to match book titles with the correct author.

Method

1 Students work individually or in pairs. Give each student/pair a copy of the handout on page 31.

2 Read through the introduction. Allow 15–20 minutes for the students to work out their answers.

3 Check the answers orally with the whole class.

Key

1 Gladys Friday (glad it's Friday), 2 L. M. N. Tree (elementary), 3 Rhoda Camel (rode a camel), 4 Andrew Pictures (Anne drew pictures), 5 T. Shott (tee shot), 6 Albert Ross (albatross), 7 R. U. Scared (are you scared?), 8 Warren Peace (war and peace), 9 Dinah Mite (dynamite), 10 M. T. Cupboard (empty cupboard), 11 Roland Butter (roll and butter), 12 Andy Mann (handyman), 13 Gail Force (gale force), 14 Robin Holmes (robbing homes), 15 L. E. Fant (elephant), 16 C. U. Later (see you later), 17 Ivor Fortune (I've a fortune), 18 Anne Tarctic (Antarctic), 19 R. E. Volting (are revolting), 20 Justin Case (just in case)

---

11 Car accident claims   *Intermediate and above*

In this activity, the students have to sort out broken sentences. They are quotations taken from genuine car accident reports sent to insurance companies.

Method

1 Students work in pairs. Give each pair a copy of the handout on page 32.

2 Read through the introduction. Allow 10–15 minutes for the students to work out their answers.

3 Check the answers orally with the whole class.

Key

1 f, 2 l, 3 o, 4 i, 5 m, 6 c, 7 n, 8 k, 9 a, 10 d, 11 h, 12 g, 13 b, 14 j, 15 e

---

12 What are they saying?   *Elementary*

This is an activity based on matching common phrases with drawings.

Method

1 Students work individually or in pairs. Give each student/pair a copy of the handout on page 33.

2 Read through the introduction and the phrases. Allow 15–20 minutes for the students to work out their answers.

3 When everyone is ready, check the answers orally with the whole class.

Key

1 f, 2 c, 3 j, 4 h, 5 b, 6 g, 7 d, 8 i, 9 e, 10 a

---

13 Cartoons 1   *Elementary*

This is an activity based on matching captions with the correct cartoon.

Method

1 Students work individually or in pairs. Give each student/pair a copy of the handout on page 34.

2 Read through the introduction and the captions. Allow 15–20 minutes for the students to work out their answers.

3 When everyone is ready, check the answers orally with the whole class.

Key

1 e, 2 h, 3 a, 4 f, 5 j, 6 d, 7 b, 8 i, 9 c, 10 g

---

14 Cartoons 2   *Intermediate*

Method

As Activity 13. The handout is on page 35.

Key

1 j, 2 f, 3 d, 4 i, 5 b, 6 e, 7 a, 8 g, 9 c, 10 h

15 Signs

This is similar to Activity 14, but this time it is based on working out which words are missing from signs.

Method
As Activity 1. The handout is on page 36.

Key
1 g, 2 i, 3 e, 4 b, 5 j, 6 h, 7 d, 8 a, 9 c, 10 f

Jigsaw reading activities

In these activities, students have to piece together or sort out texts (usually jokes) that have been mixed up in one way or another.

---

16 Sort out the joke 1
Elementary

This is a jigsaw reading activity for pairs. The students have to sort out a mixed up joke.

Method

1 There are two possible jokes to choose from at this level on page 37 or page 38. Choose one and copy it.

2 Explain to the students that they have to sort out the the joke by numbering the parts. Set a time-limit, e.g. 10–15 minutes.

3 When they have finished, check the answers by asking students to read out the joke in the correct order.

Key
Joke 1

*A man goes off on a business trip, leaving his cat with his neighbour. A few days later he phones the neighbour to ask about his pet and the neighbour says,' The cat has died.'
The poor man is very upset and says to his friend, 'Couldn't you have broken the news of my cat's death to me more gently? The first time I phoned you you could have told me that the cat was on the roof, the next time that the cat had fallen off the roof and wasn't feeling too well, and so on.'
When he came home from his business trip he got a new cat and, a few weeks later, set off on another trip. Once again, he left his cat with the same neighbour.
After a few days he phoned and asked, 'How's the cat?'
'The cat is just fine,' said his neighbour, 'but I think you should know that your mother's on the roof.'*

Joke 2

*Three tortoises go into a cafe and order three chocolate milk shakes. Then it starts to rain, so they decide that one of them should go home and fetch an umbrella.
The tortoise who offers to go is very worried that the others will drink his milk shake while he is gone. But they promise him that they won't. So he finally sets off. Two days pass and still he has not come back. Then another two days.
Finally, after a week, one of the tortoises who is still waiting says, 'I don't think he's going to come back now. Let's drink his milk shake!'*

*'Yes, I agree!' says the second tortoise.
Suddenly, the third tortoise shouts angrily from the cafe doorway, 'If you dare touch it, I won't go for the umbrella!'*

---

17 Sort out the joke 2
Intermediate
Method
As Activity 16. The handout is on page 39.

Key

*The advertisement in The Stage, a 'Showbiz' magazine read: 'Non-speaking part, but you must be very athletic.'
So Jim, being out of work, applied for the job and found himself being directed to the local Zoo. There, the zoo's director explained to him that one of the zoo's major attractions, the gorilla, had died and they needed a substitute until the real thing could be imported.
'All you have to do is wear this gorilla suit for a few weeks and swing around the branches,' said the zoo's director.
The few weeks turned into a month and, although it was hot in the suit, the pay was good. Jim had even worked out quite a good routine, leaping and tumbling about. And the public seemed to love it. Indeed the crowd's applause drove him to be even more daring until one day, while attempting a somersault he lost his grip and fell out of the tree and straight into the lion's enclosure.
When he recovered his senses he saw the lion approaching and started to scream for help.
'Shut up, you fool!' said the lion. 'Do you want to get us both the sack?'*

---

18 Sort out the joke 3
Advanced
Method
As Activity 16. The handout is on page 40.

Key

*An Englishman, a Scotsman and an Irishman were all working on the same building site together, and they always stopped at the same time to eat their packed lunches. One day the Englishman opened up his plastic lunch container and screamed, 'Oh, no, not ham sandwiches again! If I have ham sandwiches again, I'm seriously going to kill myself.'
The Scotsman opened his lunch box and, like the Englishman screamed, 'Och no – salmon sandwiches again! If the wife makes me these one more time, I'm going to kill myself.'
The Irishman then opened his lunch box and exclaimed loudly, 'Holy Mother of God! If I have cheese sandwiches once more, I tell you, I'm going to kill myself.'
Next day, lunchtime came round again. The Englishman opened his sandwiches only to find ham again. With a loud cry of 'Ham sandwiches, I can't bear them any more!' he ran along the roof of the building and flung himself off, falling ten floors to his death.
The Scotsman then opened his lunch box, found salmon sandwiches and screamed, 'Och no, salmon again. I can't bear it any more!' and in turn flung himself off the building to his death.*

3

Finally, the Irishman opened his lunch box and, faced with the prospect of Irish cheddar sandwiches yet again, he leapt off the roof to his death.
At the funeral for the three men, held a week later, the three widows were weeping together. The English wife said, 'I don't understand. I thought he liked ham.' The Scotsman's widow sobbed, 'I don't understand it either. Jock would have said something if he really didn't like salmon.' Finally the Irish wife sniffed loudly, 'I just don't understand Paddy's behaviour at all – he always made his own sandwiches!'

---

19 Sort out the joke 4

Elementary

As Activity 16. The handout is on page 41.

Method

1 Copy and cut out the handouts on page 41. Give one to Student A and one to Student B.

2 Explain to the students that they have to sort out the joke by numbering the parts. Student A can read out the sentences to Student B and vice versa but they are not allowed to look at one another's handout. Set a time-limit, e.g. 15–20 minutes.

3 When they have finished, check the answers by asking one pair to read out the joke in the correct order.

Key

Old Jake was feeling ill, so he went to see the doctor. The doctor gave him a bottle of medicine.
'This is very strong stuff,' said the doctor. 'Don't take it every day, Jake.'
The doctor wanted to make sure old Jake understood. so he said once again, 'Not every day, now. Do you know what I mean? Take it tomorrow, then skip a day, then take it the next day and skip another day, and so on.'
A month later, the doctor saw Jake's wife in the street and asked how her husband was.
'Oh, he's dead,' she said.
'Dead!' said the doctor. 'But how? Was it the medicine? Was it too strong?'
'No, the medicine wasn't that strong,' she said. 'It was all that skipping!'

---

20 Sort out the joke 5

Intermediate

Method

As Activity 19. The handouts are on page 42.

Key

Three boys called Manners, Shut-up and Trouble were playing in the woods one day, when Trouble suddenly vanished from sight! Although they looked everywhere, Shut-up and Manners were unable to find him. They ran and shouted and ran and shouted, but Trouble had managed to get himself totally lost. So Shut-up and Manners decide to go and report Trouble's disappearance to the police.

When they arrived at the police station, Manners waited outside on the steps while Shut-up went in.
'What's your name, son?' asked the policeman behind the enquiry desk.
'Shut-up,' replied the boy.
'Eh?' said the policeman, startled. 'Where's your manners?'
'Sitting outside on the steps,' replied Shut-up.
The policeman started to get angry.
'Are your looking for trouble?' he said.
'Yes,' said Shut-up. 'How did you know?'

---

21 Sort out the jokes 1

Lower-intermediate and above

In this jigsaw reading activity, students have to sort out two jokes whose lines have got mixed up. Again they work in pairs.

Method

As Activity 16. The handout is on page 43.

Key

Joke A

A man buying a camel was advised that to make it walk he should say 'Few!', to make it run he should say 'Many!' and to make it stop he should say 'Amen!'
At his first ride all went well.
'Few!' he called, and off the camel went.
'Many!' he shouted, and the camel began to run – straight for the edge of a cliff. But the new owner had forgotten the word to make the camel stop. As the cliff edge came closer and closer he called out in terror: 'Lord save me! Lord save me! Amen!'
And of course the camel stopped – right on the very edge of the precipice. Whereupon the rider wiped his brow in relief and said, 'Phew, that was clo–AAAGH!'

Joke B

Four prisoners who had shared a cell for so long knew each other's jokes so well that they gave them all numbers rather than tell them.
One day a new prisoner was put in the same cell half-way through a joke-telling session.
'89!' said the first prisoner and the other three giggled hysterically. '96!' shouted the second and there were hoots of laughter from the other three.
'192!' cried the third and the four rolled round the cell floor. The new inmate thought he would have a go.
'66!' he said. There was silence.
'42!' he tried again. Silence.
He turned to one of his cell mates and asked what he was doing wrong.
'It's not the jokes,' he was told. 'It's the way you tell them!'

22 Sort out the jokes 2 *Intermediate*

In this jigsaw reading activity, students have to sort out three jokes whose lines have got mixed up. This time the parts are arranged in a random order on the pages. Again students work in pairs.

Method

As Activity 16. The handout is on pages 44–45.

Key

Joke A

A fast train raced along the border of the biggest cattle ranch in Texas. A passenger gazed at the huge herds and when the other boundary of the ranch was reached he turned to the man beside him and said:
'What a big herd of cattle! I counted 12,224 head.'
The man looked surprised.
'Amazing!' he cried. 'I'm the owner of that ranch and I know you're exactly right. There really are 12,224 head of cattle. How did you manage to count them when we were speeding so fast?'
'Nothing to it. I just counted their legs and divided by four!'

Joke B

Driving along a country road, Henry noticed a chicken running alongside his car. He increased his speed to 50 kilometres per hour.
The chicken kept coming. Henry put his foot down on the accelerator, but the chicken still managed to keep up. When the car reached 70 kilometres per hour, the chicken passed it and turned down a dirt road. It was then that the man noticed that the chicken had three legs.
He followed it to a farm that was filled with 3-legged chickens.
'Say,' said Henry to the farmer, 'do all your chickens have three legs?'
'Yep,' replied the farmer. 'Most people like drumsticks, so we developed this breed.'
'How do they taste?' asked Henry.
'Don't rightly know,' answered the farmer. 'Haven't been able to catch one yet!'

Joke C

A man who wanted to buy a parrot went to an animal auction. He found just what he wanted – a beautiful African bird – and decided to bid for it. The bidding went higher and higher, but finally the man was the winning bidder. He went excitedly to collect his bird and suddenly remembered that he had forgotten to ask the most important question about the parrot.
'Does the parrot talk?' he asked the auctioneer anxiously.
'Of course he talks,' replied the auctioneer.
'Who do you think was bidding against you?'

23 Sort out the jokes 3 *Advanced*

This is a jigsaw reading activity for groups of 4. Students have to sort out three jokes.

Method

1 Copy and cut up the handouts on pages 46–47 – one for each student in the group (A, B, C and D).

2 Explain that they have to sort out the three jokes. Remind them that they can read out what is on their card but they are not allowed to show it to the others in the group. Set a time-limit, e.g. 10–15 minutes.

3 When they have finished, check the answers by asking each group in turn to read out part of the jokes. For example, someone in group A would read out the first part of Joke 1, then someone from group B would read out the next part, and so on.

4 Ask the groups which joke they preferred.

Key

Joke 1

An Englishman went to Ireland to do a spot of fishing. He found a suitable spot by a river and prepared to wade out into the murky water with his wellingtons. But before he did so he asked a farmer who was mending a nearby fence if the water was shallow.
'Sure, the water's shallow,' came the reply.
With this the angler walked straight into the river – and found himself up to his neck.
'You said it was shallow!' he cried as he made his way back to the river bank completely soaked.
'Well, I thought it was,' said the farmer. 'It only comes up to the waists of the ducks, and they're only twenty centimetres tall.'

Joke 2

A sportsman – a snooker player – went to the doctor saying he thought his diet wasn't healthy enough and was making him ill.
'What do you eat in the mornings?' asked the doctor.
'Snooker balls,' said the sportsman. 'Two reds, a yellow and a brown.'
'And what do you eat for lunch?'
'For lunch? Two pinks, a red and a blue.'
'And for tea?'
'Oh, for tea a black and three reds.'
'I see,' said the doctor. 'Well, it's obvious what the matter is.'
'What is it?' asked the sportsman.
'You're not getting enough greens!'

Joke 3

A motorist who had broken down on a country road was staring hopelessly into the engine when a cow came along. To his surprise, it took a long hard look under the bonnet, then said, 'It's the battery that's the problem.'
The motorist was so stunned that he ran down the road and bumped straight into a farmer who was driving some more cows into a field. He stood and listened while the motorist told him the amazing story of what had happened.
'Was she a white cow with a brown patch between her eyes?' the farmer asked.
'Yes! Yes, that's right!' cried the motorist.
'I wouldn't take any notice if I were you,' said the farmer. 'That's Daisy and she doesn't know a thing about cars!'

5

24 Sort out the punch lines 1 — *Lower-intermediate*

In this activity, the punch lines of twelve jokes are mixed up. The students have to work out which punch line goes with which joke.

Method

1 Students work in pairs. Copy the handout on page 48 – one copy for each pair.

2 Set a time-limit, e.g. 15–20 minutes.

3 When they have finished, check the answers orally with the whole group. This can be done in dialogue form, with the students reading out loud in pairs putting in the correct punch line.

Key

Joke 1 (4), Joke 2 (6), Joke 3 (5), Joke 4 (11), Joke 5 (7), Joke 6 (2), Joke 7 (9), Joke 8 (10), Joke 9 (1), Joke 10 (12), Joke 11 (3), Joke 12 (8)

25 Sort out the punch lines 2 — *Intermediate*

Method

As Activity 24. The handout is on page 49.

Key

Joke 1 (5), Joke 2 (10), Joke 3 (7), Joke 4 (11), Joke 5 (8), Joke 6 (3), Joke 7 (9), Joke 8 (12), Joke 9 (6), Joke 10 (2), Joke 11 (1), Joke 12 (4)

26 Sort out the punch lines 3 — *Lower-intermediate*

Method

1 Students work in pairs. Copy the handout on page 50 – one copy for each pair.

2 Explain that they have to unscramble the last line (the punch line) in each joke and write it down in the correct order. Also explain that the commas, full stops, capital letters, etc. are in the correct places. Set a time-limit, e.g. 15–20 minutes.

3 When they have finished, check the answers orally with the whole group. This can be done in dialogue form, with the students reading out loud in pairs.

Key

Joke 1   I want to look at the bun first.
Joke 2   It's easy when you know how.
Joke 3   Then tell them to play cards.
Joke 4   Because there wasn't time to take them off.
Joke 5   We have trains like that in this country, too.
Joke 6   There was in this one!
Joke 7   No. She forgot to give it to me.
Joke 8   Oh, the pig won't mind that.
Joke 9   Well, your worries are over.
Joke 10   But please finish the song you were singing.

27 Sort out the punch lines 4 — *Intermediate*

Method

As Activity 26. The handout is on page 51.

Key

Joke 1   No, just a few feet off the ground.
*   (Shanghai? = she hang high?)*
Joke 2   I'll have my change here, if you don't mind.
Joke 3   Those crocodiles all look the same to me.
Joke 4   By that time I was far too famous.
Joke 5   Yes, we're a very closely knit family.
Joke 6   That means you think you're a great lover!
Joke 7   If it had two I's it wouldn't be blind.
Joke 8   Isn't it amazing that we all met up!
Joke 9   Good thing you were wearing those bandages!
Joke 10   Just because you don't believe me, there's no
*   need to murder my wee brother!*

28 Sort out the captions 1 — *Elementary/ Lower-Intermediate*

Method

1 Students work individually or in pairs. Copy the handout on page 52 – one copy for each student/pair.

2 Explain to the students that they have to work out which caption goes with which cartoon. Set a time-limit, e.g. 15–20 minutes.

3 When they have finished, check the answers orally with the whole group.

Key

Cartoon 1 (4), Cartoon 2 (7), Cartoon 3 (8), Cartoon 4 (6), Cartoon 5 (1), Cartoon 6 (9), Cartoon 7 (10), Cartoon 8 (3), Cartoon 9 (5), Cartoon 10 (2)

29 Sort out the captions 2 — *Intermediate and above*

Method

As Activity 28. The handout is on page 53.

Key

Cartoon 1 (3), Cartoon 2 (7), Cartoon 3 (6), Cartoon 4 (2), Cartoon 5 (9), Cartoon 6 (4), Cartoon 7 (10), Cartoon 8 (5), Cartoon 9 (1), Cartoon 10 (8)

30 Find the differences — *Intermediate and above*

Method

1 Students work in pairs. Copy the handouts on page 54 (Student A) and on page 55 (Student B).

2 Divide the class into pairs – A and B. Give each student a copy of the appropriate handout.

3 The students then sit facing each other, making sure that their handout is hidden from their partner.

4 Explain to the students that they have to find at least ten differences in the story. Allow time for the students to read and understand the story. Students then begin to ask and answer questions to try and find the differences.

5 Set a time-limit, e.g. 15–20 minutes.

6 Students now compare their texts to see if they managed to find all the differences.

key

line 1 - grandmother/auntie
line 1 - old/old-fashioned
line 2 - house/flat
line 2 - 10 o'clock/11 o'clock

line 2 - Saturday/Friday
line 3 - Gran/The aunt
line 3 - do some shopping/visit the library
line 5 - efficient/intelligent
line 6 - tiles on the fireplace/ornaments on the mantelpiece
line 6 - forty-five/fifty-five
line 7 - taking it apart/repairing it
line 8 - 11.30/11.40
line 9 - cigarette/cup of tea
line 11 - happy/pleased
line 12 - gassed/poisoned
line 12 - copper wire/string
line 14 - a car pulling up/the front door opening
line 16 - A few minutes later/Ten minutes later
line 16 - living-room/lounge
line 16 - fireplace/two men
line 17 - in the corner/near the window
line 17 - pale/bright red
line 18 - deeply shocked/amazed
line 19 - earlier that morning/during the night

31 Cartoon strip
Elementary

Method

1 Students work in pairs. Copy the handout on page 56 – one for each pair.

2 Explain to the students that they have to work out which words go with which drawing in the cartoon strip. Set a time-limit, e.g. 15 minutes.

3 When they have finished, check the answers orally with the whole group.

Key
Drawing 1 (3), Drawing 2 (6), Drawing 3 (8), Drawing 4 (7), Drawing 5 (4), Drawing 6 (2), Drawing 7 (1), Drawing 8 (5)

32 Right word – wrong place
Advanced

Method

1 Students work in pairs. Copy the handout on page 57 – one for each pair.

2 Explain to the students that in each joke, one, possibly two of the words have got mixed up with one of the other jokes. Students have to (a) find the wrong words and (b) say which word or words from another joke should have been used instead. Tell the students that they are looking for 10 pairs of words in total.

3 Set a time-limit, e.g. 15 minutes. When they have finished, check the answers orally with the whole group by reading out the jokes, this time with the correct words.

Key

Joke	Wrong word	Correct word	Joke
1	stealing	missing	7
1	recently	probably	10
2	number	drum	7
3	distressed	impressed	6
3	outlaws	figures	12
4	cannibal	driver	9
5	approached	thanked	6
5	real	amazing	11
8	tourists	kittens	12
8	broken	whole	10

Misprints and more activities

In this section, the activities are based on misprints and humorous translations.

33 Misprints 1
Elementary/Lower-Intermediate

This activity is based on newspaper misprints. The students have to find the misprint in each story and correct it.

Method

1 Students work alone or in pairs. Copy the handout on page 58 – one for each student/pair in the class.

2 Read through the introduction and the example. Allow 15–20 minutes for the students to work out their answers.

3 When everyone is ready, check the answers orally with the whole class.

Key

	Wrong word	Correct word
1	*honey*	*money*
2	*eating*	*beating*
3	*hell*	*held*
4	*fights*	*flights*
5	*fat*	*flat*
6	*car*	*cat*
7	*gin*	*gun*
8	*bear*	*beard*
9	*sing*	*sign*
10	God	Dog
11	*officers*	*offices*
12	*dead*	*deaf*
13	*nose*	*rose*
14	Crows	Crowds
15	Window	Widow

34 Misprints 2
Intermediate

Method

As Activity 33. The handout is on page 59.

Key

	Wrong word	Correct word
1	*thorn*	*throne*
2	*bust*	*bus*
3	*ship*	*hip*
4	*bare*	*bear*
5	*wee*	*week*
6	*wind*	*wine*
7	*unclear*	*nuclear*
8	*ballet*	*ballot*
9	*curses*	*courses*
10	*rabbi*	*rabbit*
11	*polite*	*police*
12	*pants*	*plants*
13	*pets*	*pests*
14	*purse*	*pulse*
15	*sit*	*set*

35 Misprints 3 *Advanced*

Method

As Activity 33. The handout is on page 60.

Key

	Wrong word	Correct word
1	nasty	tasty
2	strangler	stranger
3	pretty	petty
4	battle-scared	battle-scarred
5	raided	raised
6	rape	wrap
7	fight	night
8	peasant	pleasant
9	tickling	tackling
10	fish	fist
11	socks	stocks
12	die	dine
13	defective	detective
14	treat	threat
15	scar	car

36 More than one meaning 1 *Advanced*

This is an activity based on ambiguous sentences and headlines. The students have to try to explain the 'unexpected' meaning.

Method

1 Students work in pairs. Copy the handout on page 61 – one for each pair.

2 Read through the introduction and, if necessary, go through the first example with the whole class. The students work with their partner, taking it in turns to explain the ambiguity in the sentences or headlines.

3 When everyone has finished, check the answers orally with the whole class.

Key

Possible answers:

1 *It is bad manners to physically roll in your soup.*
2 *The crowd were very happy that his speech was short.*
3 *Cancer is linked to smoking in a room – a study.*
4 *You can eat children for £3.50.*
5 *The judge gave him another chance to strangle his wife.*
6 *Sword fencing in a swimming pool can save a child's life.*
7 *Let me clean you, i.e. your body.*
8 *It is the cow that doesn't smoke or drink.*
9 *They didn't need their husbands.*
10 *The bikinis only have tops – no bottoms.*
11 *There is a physical crack (not the drug crack) in the continent.*
12 *They eat the restaurant owner before they rob him.*
13 *A car is to talk on Friday.*
14 *They have been in the checkout queue for 18 years.*
15 *The farmer has two heads.*
16 *She was born at the age of 88.*
17 *Pets are allowed to bury their owners.*
18 *The bears were driving.*
19 *The bulldog loves eating children.*
20 *John Lennon was killed during the interview.*

37 More than one meaning 2 *Advanced*

Method

As Activity 36. The handout is on page 62.

Key

(Possible answers for 'alternative' meaning)

1 *His own death was the turning point in his (i.e. the Prime Minister's) life.*
2 *The baby's chair can be made into all these things, including an Elvis Presley CD!*
3 *The dress fell off as she walked down the aisle.*
4 *Men don't strike (= hit) women as often as migraines do.*
5 *Their bodies are turning to powder.*
6 *It was the Surrey police who stole the cars.*
7 *It was the psychiatrist who had a severe emotional problem.*
8 *His parents murdered him.*
9 *It is considered healthy to kick a baby.*
10 *His leg had been physically hanging over his head (which must have been very inconvenient for him and made walking difficult).*
11 *The oil covered rocks were walking along the shore.*
12 *He had a baseball bat hidden in his underwear.*
13 *The toilet is 5 miles from Epsom.*
14 *He will take (i.e. steal) anything.*
15 *The original body (of the dead person) is still in the hearse.*
16 *Lenin's body physically moved. (Perhaps his leg moved)*
17 *The astronauts will vomit (i.e. bring up their breakfasts) soon.*
18 *Her husband has been buried at the cemetery more than once.*
19 *In New York you are not allowed to box after you die.*
20 *You can use platforms 7–8 as toilets.*

38 Strange but true! *Intermediate and above*

These are examples of sentences which, although grammatically correct, are strange in some way because of their content. In this activity students fill in missing words.

Method

1 Students work alone or in pairs. Copy the handout on page 63 – one for each student/pair.

2 Explain to the students that they have to fill the gaps in the sentences with a word from the box. Tell them that not all the words will be used. Allow 15–20 minutes for the students to complete the activity.

3 When everyone has finished check the answers orally with the whole class.

Key

*1 corpse, 2 housewife, 3 remember, 4 pierced, 5 wooden,
6 suicide, 7 black and white, 8 result, 9 studied, 10 repair,
11 leaflets, 12 requires, 13 last, 14 winner, 15 Ireland,
16 wear … nose … blue, 17 take place, 18 photo, 19 bullet,
20 grapes, 21 feel*

39 Silly signs 1 *Intermediate and above*

Method

1 Students work alone or in pairs. Copy the handout on page 64 – one for each student/pair.

2 Explain to the students that the signs have words missing. They have to complete the signs with the words in the box. Tell them that not all the words will be used. Allow 15–20 minutes for the students to complete the activity.

3 When everyone has finished. Check the answers orally with the whole class.

Key

*1 regret, 2 dogs, 3 except, 4 waitress … enough,
5 guarantee, 6 customer, 7 send, 8 not … bar,
9 feed … guard, 10 other, 11 door, 12 lost*

40 Silly signs 2 *Intermediate and above*

Method

As Activity 39. The handout is on page 65.

Key

*1 sold, 2 feet, 3 on account of, 4 sleeps, 5 neatly,
6 instant … prosecuted, 7 out of order, 8 problem … should,
9 singing, 10 while … Pay, 11 spoken,
12 complaints … most*

41 Courtroom English *Lower-Intermediate and above*

This activity is based on real transcripts from a courtroom. Students have to complete the dialogues with words from the box.

Method

As Activity 39. The handout is on page 66.

Key

*1 describe, 2 height, 3 recognise, 4 present, 5 commit,
6 successful, 7 relationship, 8 acquainted, 9 married,
10 husband, 11 identify, 12 stood back, 13 gun*

42 Excuses, etc. *Intermediate and above*

Method

As Activity 39. The handout is on page 67.

Key

*1 ever since, 2 knee, 3 no longer, 4 refused, 5 given birth,
6 enclosed, 7 annoyed, 8 married, 9 changed,
10 difference, 11 pay, 12 unable, 13 late, 14 until, 15 absent,
16 proceedings, 17 yell, 18 psychiatrist*

Text activities

As the title suggests, in this section the emphasis is on manipulating texts (i.e. jokes, amusing stories, etc.) in some way, usually with the students working in pairs or groups.

43 Expand a text *Intermediate*

Method

1 Copy the handout on page 68 – one for each pair.

2 Tell the students that they have to decide where in the joke the six missing words go. (They will probably have to read through the joke several times before they can work out where the words go.)

3 When everyone has finished, check the answers orally with the whole class.

Key

NB: Some students may come up with answers which differ from the key. If they are syntactically correct, they should be accepted.

Expected answer

*Two men were climbing a particularly difficult mountain when one of them suddenly fell down a crevasse 500 feet deep.
'Are you all right Bert?' called the man at the top of the crevasse.
'I'm still alive, thank goodness, Fred,' came the reply.
'Here, grab this rope,' said Fred, throwing a rope down to Bert.
'I can't grab it,' shouted Bert. 'My arms are broken.'
'Well, fit it round your legs.'
'I'm afraid I can't do that either ,' apologized Bert. 'My legs are broken.'
'Put the rope in your mouth,' shouted Fred.
So Bert put the rope in his mouth and Fred began to haul him to safety: 490 feet … 400 feet … 300 feet … 200 feet … 100 feet … 50 feet … and then Fred called: 'Are you all right, Bert?'
'Yeh-h-h…h…h…'*

Acknowledgement: This activity is based on an idea by Simon Greenall in TOP CLASS ACTIVITIES 1. published by Penguin Books, 1997.

44 Shorten a text 1 — *Lower-Intermediate*

Method

1 Copy and cut out the handout on page 69 – one for each pair.

2 Tell the students that the joke has a number of words which can be crossed out without losing the general sense. Ask them to read the joke and cross out five words without altering the sense of it. They will probably have to read through the joke several times before they can work out where the words are.

3 When everyone has finished, check the answers orally with the whole class.

Key

NB: Some students may come up with answers which differ from the key. If they are syntactically correct, they should be accepted.

Expected answers

An Englishman, an Irishman and a (tall) Scotsman were hiding from (armed) bandits up (palm) trees. The bandit chief called up one tree, 'Who's there?' And the Englishman went 'Cheep! Cheep!' (loudly), like a bird. So the bandit chief called up the next tree, 'Who's there?' And the Scotsman went 'Eeek! Eeek!' (just) like a monkey. So the bandit chief called up the next tree, 'Who's there?' And the Irishman went, 'Moo–oo!

Acknowledgement: This activity is based on an idea by Simon Greenall in TOP CLASS ACTIVITIES 1. published by Penguin Books, 1997.

---

45 Shorten a text 2 — *Intermediate*

Method

As Activity 44. The handout is on page 69.

Key

Expected answers

On the street stood a (middle-aged) man, a dog and a (black) horse. The dog was playing an accordion while the horse sang (beautifully), and the man was collecting money from passers-by. One (old) lady stopped and remarked on what an amazing sight the three made.
'And how (very) talented you are. You should be performing in a circus.'
'(Oh) no, madam,' said the man (seriously), 'my conscience wouldn't let me do that. I'll let you into a secret, though. The horse can't (really) sing. The dog's a ventriloquist, (actually)!'

Acknowledgement: This activity is based on an idea by Simon Greenall in TOP CLASS ACTIVITIES 1. published by Penguin Books, 1997.

---

46 One word only — *Intermediate*

Method

1 Students work individually or in pairs. Copy the handout on page 70 – one for each student/pair.

2 Tell the students that the joke has a number of words missing. Their task is to suggest suitable words for each blank. They can only use one word for each blank. Let them look at the example first. Set a time-limit, e.g. 20 minutes.

3 When everyone has finished, check orally with the whole class.

Key

Suggested answers

(1) left (2) not/never/seldom/rarely (3) next (4) How (5) ups (6) as/with (7) branch/office (8) sounds/is (9) done/fared/been (10) married/wed (11) within/after (12) of (13) too (14) buying (15) into (16) walk (17) against (18) either (19) run (20) fire (21) mind (22) living (23) luck

---

47 Choose the answer 1 — *Elementary*

This is a multiple-choice exercise where students have to choose the best word or words that fit into the blanks in a joke. Again, students can work individually or in pairs.

Method

1 Copy the handout on page 71 – one copy for each student/pair.

2 Tell the students that the joke has a number of blanks and for each blank there is a choice of four different words. Their task is to decide which word or words is best for each blank. Let them look at the example first before they try the activity themselves. Set a time-limit, e.g. 15–20 minutes.

3 When everyone is finished, check the answers orally with the whole class.

Key

1 c, 2 a, 3 b, 4 d, 5 c, 6 a, 7 c, 8 b, 9 a, 10 b, 11 d, 12 d, 13 b

---

48 Choose the answer 2 — *Intermediate*

Method

As Activity 47. The handout is on page 72.

Key

1 c, 2 a, 3 b, 4 d, 5 b, 6 d, 7 a, 8 c, 9 b, 10 c, 11 a, 12 b, 13 a, 14 d, 15 d, 16 c

---

49 Fill in the verbs 1 — *Lower-Intermediate*

Method

1 Copy the handout on page 73 – one copy for each student/pair.

2 Tell the students that the joke has a number of blanks where various verbs are missing. Explain that after each section they have a list of verbs to choose from, but not all of these will be used! The students also have to put the verb into the correct tense. Set a time-limit, e.g. 15–20 minutes.

3 When everyone has finished, check orally with the whole class.

Key

1 escaped, 2 arrested, 3 tried, 4 open, 5 believe, 6 walked, 7 deposit, 8 had stolen, 9 told, 10 was, 11 wanted, 12 put, 13 was, 14 tried, 15 force, 16 steal, 17 woke up, 18 beat, 19 grabbed, 20 took, 21 arrested, 22 got

---

50 Fill in the verbs 2 *Intermediate*

Method

As Activity 49. The handout is on page 74.

Key

1 arrested, 2 selling, 3 claimed, 4 produce, 5 confiscated, 6 had been, 7 told, 8 confuse, 9 marking, 10 correct, 11 complained, 12 work, 13 advertised, 14 seemed, 15 turned up, 16 left, 17 took, 18 saw, 19 turned out, 20 lived, 21 had offered, 22 was sentenced, 23 had confessed

---

51 Fill in the verbs 3 *Advanced*

Method

As Activity 49. The handout is on page 75.

Key

1 came, 2 Performing, 3 finished off, 4 catching, 5 fired, 6 produced, 7 had hidden, 8 missed, 9 took out, 10 yelling, 11 fired, 12 blowing, 13 had killed, 14 made, 15 understand, 16 caught, 17 sympathised, 18 acquitted, 19 was found, 20 carrying, 21 received, 22 put

---

52 Find the mistakes *Intermediate and above*

Students work in pairs.

Method

1 Copy the handout on page 76 – one for each pair.

2 Tell the students that some of the lines in the joke are correct while some have a word that should not be there. It is up to the students to decide which lines are correct and which lines are incorrect.   Before starting, look through the two examples to make sure the students understand what they have to do. Set a time-limit, e.g. 20 minutes.

3 When everyone has finished, check orally with the whole class.

Key

1 the, 2✓, 3✓, 4 up, 5✓, 6✓, 7✓, 8 a, 9 was, 10✓, 11✓, 12 after, 13 had, 14✓, 15✓, 16 himself, 17 away, 18 to, 19✓, 20✓

---

53 Can you read it? *Intermediate and above*

This is a vocabulary cloze activity. The students can work individually or in pairs.

Method

1 Copy the handout on page 77 – one for each student/pair.

2 Tell the students that they have to read the letter from the skeleton given and fill in the missing letters. Explain that each dash is one missing letter. Set a time-limit, e.g. 20 minutes.

3 When everyone has finished, check the answers orally with the whole class by asking the students to take turns at reading the sentences out loud.

Key

Letter from a loving mother

Dear son,
Just a few lines to let you know I'm still alive. I'm writing this letter slowly because I know you can't read fast. You won't know the house when you get home because we have moved.
About your father. He has a lovely new job. He has five hundred men under him. He cuts grass at the cemetery. There was a washing machine in the new house when we moved in but it hasn't been working too well. Last week I put Dad's shirt in, pulled the chain and haven't seen it since.
Your sister, Mary, had a baby this morning but I haven't found out if it's a boy or a girl yet, so I don't know if you are an aunt or an uncle.
I went to the doctor last Thursday and your father came with me. The doctor put a small glass tube in my mouth and told me not to talk for ten minutes. Your father offered to buy it off him.
It only rained twice this week, first for three days and then for four.
We had a letter from the undertaker. He said if the last payment on your grandfather's plot isn't paid within seven days, then up he comes.

Your loving mother.

P.S.
I was going to send you £10 but I had already sealed up the envelope.

---

54 Sort out the missing words *Intermediate and above*

This is a reading activity where students have to decide where a number of missing phrases go in a joke. Students can work individually or in pairs.

Method

1 Copy the handout on page 78 – one for each student/pair.

2 Tell the students that fifteen phrases have been left out of the joke. Their task is to choose the correct phrase from the 18 given for each gap. Do the first one with the whole class then let them complete the rest. Set a time-limit, e.g. 20–25 minutes.

3 Check orally with the whole class.

Key

*1 q, 2 c, 3 i, 4 b, 5 m, 6 k, 7 e, 8 d, 9 f, 10 n, 11 j, 12 a,
13 g, 14 h, 15 r*

---

55 What's missing?   *Intermediate*

This is a reading/cloze activity. It is best done in pairs.

Method

1 Copy the handout on page 79 – one for each pair.

2 Tell the students that some of the lines in the joke are
correct while some have a word missing. It is up to the
students to decide which lines are correct and which
lines have a word missing. Before starting, look through
the two examples to make sure the students understand
what they have to do. Set a time-limit, e.g. 20–25
minutes.

3 Check orally with the whole class.

Key

*1✓, 2 and (up/down), 3✓, 4✓, 5 across, over, down, along
(wandered/the), 6 was (which/crying), 7✓, 8 ran, walked,
hurried (I/bravely), 9 did (What/you), 10 ✓,
11 Could/Would/Will (/You tell), 12✓, 13 Where (/Are you),
14✓, 15✓, 16 to (off/the), 17 said (and/to), 18✓, 19 here
(staying/), 20✓, 21✓, 22 have, hire (I/her), 23 then
(Just/the), 24✓, 25 who, that (/pushed)*

Miscellaneous activities

This is a general collection of various sorts of activities –
including a number of single sheet handouts to be
filled in.

---

56 Booking a room at a hotel   *All*

This is a fun activity for groups of six students.

Method

1 Copy the dialogue on page 80 – two copies for each
group. Also copy and cut up the acting cards on page 81
– one set per group.

2 Give each group two copies of the dialogue plus the
acting cards. These are shuffled and placed face down on
the table. Each student takes a card and makes sure no
one else in the group sees it!

3 Students take it in turns to act out the dialogue in pairs.
The person playing the hotel receptionist (A) reads the
part 'straight'. The other person (B) reads the part
according to the acting card s(he) has picked up. The
others listen and, at the end, try to guess what acting
instructions B had been given.

4 Continue until everyone has played the part of B.

5 When everyone has finished, why not ask for one or two
volunteers to act it out in front of the class?

57 Explain yourself!   *Lower-Intermediate
and above*

This is a fun activity for small groups of 3–4 students.

Method

1 Copy and cut out the ten sentences ('situations') on
page 82.

2 Divide the class into small groups, 3–4 students per
group.

3 Give a situation to each group. Tell them they now have
5 minutes to come up with a suitable explanation.

4 Taking it in turns, one person from each group reads
out their situation and gives an explanation. The rest of
the class now decide whether to accept it or not.
Encourage the students to interrupt and cross-examine
the person talking!

---

58 Carry on talking   *Lower-Intermediate
and above*

This is a pair activity where students are given the opening
lines of a dialogue and have to continue it for as long as
possible.

Method

1 Copy and cut out the six dialogues on page 83. (Make
enough copies so that each pair in the class gets one of
them.)

2 Divide the class into pairs and give each pair a dialogue.

3 Explain that these are the opening words of a dialogue.
Tell them to decide who will be A and B, then to see how
long they can continue the dialogue.

4 Set a time-limit, e.g. 15 minutes, then get one or two
pairs to act out their dialogue for the rest of the class.

5 You could ask the students to write up their dialogue for
homework.

---

59 Consequences   *All*

This is a group activity based on a familiar game and can
often give amusing results.

Method

1 Give each student a copy of the handout on page 84.

2 Tell them all to write down first the name of a well-
known man, then to fold their paper so that the name is
now hidden.

3 They pass their papers to the person on their left and
next write down the name of a well-known woman.
Again, they fold the paper and pass it on.

4 Continue like this until all ten items have been filled in.

5 Each person now reads out the final story. It can often
be very amusing!

6 Finally, each group can choose their funniest
'Consequences sheet' and take it in turns to read them
out to the whole class.

60 Half a crossword
Lower-Intermediate

In this activity, the students work in two groups A and B. Each group has an incomplete crossword. By asking for and miming definitions, they try to fill in the missing words.

Method

1 Copy the crossword on page 85 (Group A) and on page 86 (Group B).

2 Divide the class into A and B groups of 2–3 students per group. They sit facing each other. Give each group a copy of the crossword and, before starting, allow them time to check through the words they will have to mime.

NOTE: On no account must they let the other group see their crossword!

3 Explain that they have to take it in turns to ask for a word that is missing from their crossword. They simply ask What's 1 Down? What's 4 Across? etc. The other group now have to try to mime the word as best they can. They are not allowed to speak other than make noises, e.g. the grunting of a pig. (Anyone in the group can mime.)

4 Set a definite time-limit and stop the students at the end of it whether they have finished or not.

5 They can now compare their crosswords and check any words they didn't fill in.

6 You can follow up by asking the groups to demonstrate how they mimed one or two of the more difficult words.

61 Tongue-twisters
Lower-Intermediate

A lot of fun can be had from trying to read out tongue-twisters. This is a group contest based on tongue-twisters.

Method

1 Copy and cut out the tongue twister cards on page 87 – one set for each group.

2 The tongue-twister cards are shuffled and placed face down on the table. One player starts. S(he) picks up the top card and tries to say it three times as quickly as possible. If the others think s(he) has said it well (s)he keeps the card. If not, the person on his/her right has a go. If successful s(he) keeps the card. If not play proceeds until everyone in the group has tried. If no one is successful at the end, the card is discarded and the next one turned up.

3 Play continues in this manner. Set a time-limit (approx. 15 minutes).

4 The person with the most cards at the end wins.

Variation

It can also be played as a team game, with three students acting as judges.

1 Divide the class into four teams (6 students per team). Have four copies of the cards, arranged on the table in the same order.

2 One person from each team comes out to the front. They are all given the same tongue-twister and allowed 1 minute to look at it before starting. Then they take it in turns to read out their tongue-twister three times, after which the three judges say who said it best. (If the judges cannot agree, the teacher will have to arbitrate.) The winner gets 10 points.

3 The team with the highest points at the end of 6 rounds wins.

(NOTE: If the class is larger or smaller, adjust the team sizes and number of rounds accordingly.)

62 Test your logic
Lower-intermediate and above

This is an activity for pairs which tests how logically the students can think.

Method

1 Copy the handout on page 88 – one copy per pair.

2 The students read through the questions and write down their answers. Set a time-limit of 15–20 minutes..

3 Check orally by asking different pairs in turn for their answers.

Key:

1 Because he/she isn't dead. 2 All of them. 3 11. The daughter is each son's sister. 4 You don't bury survivors as they aren't dead. 5 (c) her daughter, 6 It was still Mount Everest. 7 The match. 8 Nine. 9 16, 515. 10 There are no stairs in a bungalow (suggested answer).
11 Three. 12 No one. Peacocks (males) can't lay eggs.
13 a chair, a bed, a toothbrush, 14 Once. 15 It was still daylight. 16 Neither. 9 + 7 = 16. 17 Dead.

63 Complete the crossword
Lower-Intermediate

This is a crossword activity for pairs where the missing words in three jokes form the clues for the crossword.

Method

1 Copy the handout on page 89 – one copy per pair.

2 Explain what the students have to do. If you like, do the first example with them. Set a time-limit, e.g. 20 minutes.

3 Check orally by reading through the jokes and pausing before each missing word.

Key:

Across
3 and, 5 more, 6 anything, 8 should, 11 everything, 12 left, 16 second, 18 arrived, 19 time, 20 who, 21 still, 22 having

Down
1 they, 2 until, 4 said, 5 moment, 7 times, 9 holiday, 10 there, 13 when, 14 asked, 15 brought, 17 course, 19 talk, 20 went

64 Knock-Knock jokes
Lower-Intermediate

This is an activity for groups based on Knock-Knock jokes.

Method

1 Copy and cut out the Knock-Knock cards on page 90 – one set per group.
2 Before starting, demonstrate a Knock-Knock joke. Write the pattern on the board, namely:

A: Knock, knock.
B: Who's there?
A: ____
B: Who?
A: ____

3 Use this joke to demonstrate: Knock knock. Who's there? Isabel. Isabel who? Isabell really necessary on a bicycle?

4 Give out the cards and tell the group to place them face down on the desk/table in front of them. They now take it in turns to pick up a card and go through the above 'Knock-knock' sequence. When they have done one, they decide whether to 'keep' the joke (if it is good) or reject it. Set a time-limit, e.g. 15–20 minutes.

3 Ask them to look at the pile of jokes they have kept and to choose their favourite one. See how many groups chose the same one.

---

65 Pelmanism: waiter jokes
Intermediate and above

This is an activity for pairs based on the popular game 'pelmanism' or 'memory' and is based on 2-line waiter jokes.

Method

1 Copy and cut out the 15 customer cards on page 91 and the 15 waiter cards on page 92 – one set for each pair. (NOTE: If possible, print the cards on different coloured paper.)

2 Give out the cards and tell each pair to shuffle them separately, and to place the customer cards on the table face down on the left, and the waiter cards face down on the right. Like this:

Customer cards			Waiter cards		
1	2	3	1	2	3.
4	5	6	4	5	6
7	8	9	7	8	9
10	11	12	10	11	12
13	14	15	13	14	15

3 They now take it in turns to pick up a customer card, read it out, then a waiter card and read it out. If they are a matching pair (i.e. it's the correct joke) the player removes the card from the board. If not, the cards are turned over and it's the next player's turn.

4 Carry on like this for about 20 minutes. The player with the most matching pairs at the end is the winner.

(NOTE: They are arranged in the book in the correct order, to make it easy to check which question goes with which answer. It also helps if the students sit side by side facing the cards than opposite each other.)

Part 2

Material for photocopying

1 HAVE YOU HEARD THE ONE ABOUT…?

'Do you serve foreigners?' asked the man in the pub.
'Of course we do, sir,' replied the barman.
'Right. A pint of beer for me and two foreigners for my crocodile here.'

Name	Points	Name	Points

A farmer said to his wife, 'We've been married fifty years. Why don't we kill the chicken tonight?'
His wife said, 'Why kill the chicken. It's not his fault.'

Name	Points	Name	Points

Did you hear about the well-behaved little boy? Whenever he was good, his dad gave him 10p and a pat on the head. By the time he was sixteen, he had £786 and a flat head.

Name	Points	Name	Points

A visitor was really impressed by the production chart on the wall of a Russian factory. '5,000 THE FIRST YEAR, 50,000 THE NEXT, 500,000 THIS YEAR.'
'You'll be up to a million soon. What do you make?'
'Out-of-order notices.'

Name	Points	Name	Points

A man bought a bath and was just leaving the shop with his purchase when the shop assistant called:
'Do you want a plug?'
'Why?' asked the man. 'Is it electric?'

Name	Points	Name	Points

On the day of the wedding, a woman wearing an enormous flowery hat was stopped at the entrance to the church. 'Are you a friend of the bride?' asked the usher. 'Of course not!' snapped the woman. 'I'm the groom's mother.'

Name	Points	Name	Points

A farmer was surprised to see his friend playing poker with his sheepdog. 'I know sheepdogs are intelligent,' he said, 'but that's one's brilliant.'
'Oh, he's not that good,' answered his friend. 'Every time he gets a good hand he wags his tail.'

Name	Points	Name	Points

The track official approached the new athlete.
'Are you a pole vaulter?'
'Yes,' he replied. 'I am from Gdansk. But how did you know my name vas Valter?'

Name	Points	Name	Points

A man with a pig under his arm approached the hotel reception desk.
'Where did you get that?' asked the receptionist.
'I won it in a raffle,' answered the pig.

Name	Points	Name	Points

I once went to a sale and bought a very old and very large bureau. While I was cleaning it, I must have pressed a secret button and a large panel in the back of the bureau popped open and three people fell out shouting, 'Where am I? Where am I?' That's how I realised I must have bought a missing person's bureau.

Name	Points	Name	Points

Sammy was walking down the street with two bricks under his arm. 'What are you doing with those bricks?' his friend asked.
'I'm going to Harry's house. He put a brick through my window last night.' 'But why the two bricks?' he was asked.
'Well, you see, he's got double glazing.'

Name	Points		Name	Points

A girl was given some pills by the doctor to help her lose weight before her wedding. A few days later she returned. 'These pills have terrible side effects, doctor,' she said. 'They make me feel very aggressive. Why, the other night I actually bit off my boyfriend's ear.'
'Don't worry, that'll only be about 60 calories or so.'

Name	Points		Name	Points

The motorist pulled up a few yards down the road, got out of the car and ran back to the scene of the accident.
'What's the matter with you? Are you blind?' asked the pedestrian, picking himself up from the road.
'Blind, what do you mean, blind?' asked the motorist. 'I hit you, didn't I?'

Name	Points		Name	Points

'I have some good news and some bad news,' said the doctor. 'First the good news. You're very sick and have only 24 hours to live.'
'You call that good news?' sobbed the patient. 'I have only 24 hours to live? What could be worse than that?'
'I should have told you yesterday!'

Name	Points		Name	Points

Jock, from Scotland, was telling his friends all about his trip to London. 'It's a lovely place,' he said, 'but they have some really strange customs. Every night the people in the rooms around mine knocked on the walls, on the ceiling, sometimes even on the floor. I could hardly hear my bagpipes!'

Name	Points		Name	Points

Robin Hood was very seriously wounded during a battle outside Nottingham Castle. His Merry Men hid him in a very small cottage. As he lay dying they said to him, 'Speak to us Robin, speak to us.' He said, 'Give me a bow and arrow, and where the arrow falls, bury me.' So he shot an arrow – and they buried him on top of the wardrobe.

Name	Points		Name	Points

The removal man was struggling to get a large wardrobe up the stairs.
'Why don't you get Charlie to help you?' asked the foreman, to which the removal man answered,
'He's inside carrying the clothes.'

Name	Points		Name	Points

My brother said, 'Mum, can I saw my sister in half?'
My mum said, 'What do you want to do that for?'
My brother said, 'Well, I've always wanted a half sister.'

Name	Points		Name	Points

Two men met after not seeing each other for many years. One said to the other, 'I hear your first two wives died of eating poisoned mushrooms, and now your third has just fallen off a cliff. That's a bit odd, isn't it?'
'Not at all,' said the second man. 'She wouldn't eat the mushrooms.'

Name	Points		Name	Points

A country girl who could neither read nor write used to sign for her wages with a cross. One Friday she came in and, instead of signing with the cross as usual, she drew a circle.
'Why don't you make your cross?' asked the farmer.
'Well, I got married last week,' she answered, 'and I've changed my name.'

Name	Points		Name	Points

2 TWO-LINE JOKES 1

What was the tortoise doing on the motorway?	About ten metres an hour.
What did the big chimney say to the little chimney?	You're too young to smoke.
What did the traffic light say to the car?	Don't look now, I'm changing.
What's worse than finding a worm in an apple?	Finding half a worm.
Do you know that it takes three sheep to make a sweater?	Really? I didn't even know they could knit.
What's the new baby's name?	I don't know. We can't understand a word he says.
You smell good. What have you got on?	Clean socks.
Can you stand on your head?	No, it's too high.
Am I the first girl you ever kissed?	Could be. Were you in Hastings in 1982.
Do people fall off the Empire State Building often?	No, only once

How do you know when there's an elephant under the bed?	Your nose touches the ceiling.
I say, driver, do you stop at the Ritz Hotel?	What, on my wages?
I broke my arm in three places.	Well, you ought to stay out of those places then!
How can you tell a British workman by his hands?	They're always in his pocket.
What do you call a crocodile at the North Pole?	Lost.
Do you write with your left hand or your right hand?	Neither – I use a ballpoint pen.
You've put your shoes on the wrong feet.	But these are the only feet I've got, Mum!
How do you get a man to stop biting his nails?	Make him wear his shoes.
Why were the two flies playing football in a saucer?	They were practising for the cup.
Why do golfers take an extra pair of trousers with them?	In case they get a hole in one.

3 TWO-LINE JOKES 2

What did the big telephone say to the little telephone?	You're too young to be engaged.
I'm losing my memory. It's got me terribly worrried.	Never mind. Try to forget about it.
My new baby looks like me.	Well, never mind. As long as it's healthy.
How come you were born in Copenhagen?	I wanted to be near my mother.
What do you do for a living?	As little as possible.
You missed school yesterday, didn't you?	No, sir, not a bit.
Eight out of ten people write with a ballpoint pen.	What do the other two do with it?
It cost me £5,000 to have my house painted.	Wouldn't it have been cheaper to have it photographed?
If we did get engaged, would you give me a ring?	Of course. What's your number?
Where was the Declaration of Independence signed?	At the bottom.

Tell me little boy, how do you like school?	Closed.
And what will you do when you're as big as your mother?	Go on a diet.
Excuse me, could you tell me the way to Bath?	Well, I always use soap and water.
Are you a mechanic?	No, I'm a McDonald.
When is the best time to pick strawberries?	When the farmer isn't looking.
Are the car indicators working?	Yes, no, yes, no, yes, no, yes ...
What's lighter than a feather but much harder to hold?	Your breath.
I've decided to race pigeons.	You'll never win. They've got wings.
Where's the best place to go when you're dying?	The living-room.
What's the quickest way to get to the hospital?	Stand in the middle of the fast lane of a motorway.

4 TWO-LINE JOKES 3

What do you get when you cross a sheep with a kangaroo?	A woolly jumper.
What goes putt ... putt ... putt ... putt ... putt ... putt?	A bad golfer.
Why did the burglar take a bath?	So he could make a clean getaway.
Have your eyes ever been checked?	No, they've always been blue.
The truth is, I regret the day I was married.	You're lucky. I was married a whole month.
Will you join me in a bowl of soup?	Is it big enough for the both of us?
How many ears did Davy Crockett have?	A left ear, a right ear and wild frontier.
Can I have a goldfish for my son?	Sorry, sir, we don't do swaps.
What goes 'tick, tock, woof'?	A watchdog.
What has four legs and flies?	A dead horse.

What do you call a man who has lost 90 per cent of his brain?	A widower.
What did the adding machine say to the clerk?	You can count on me.
I want a job as a human cannonball.	I bet you get fired.
Shall I put the stamp on myself?	No, on the letter.
Do you have any trouble making decisions?	Yes and no.
What's the best answer for water on the brain?	A tap on the head.
Is this letter for you? The name's all smudged.	No, my name's Jones.
How can you help a starving cannibal?	Give him a hand.
Are your curtains drawn?	No, they're real.
What should you do if your nose is on strike?	Picket.

5   BECAUSE ...1

Why do giraffes have such long necks?	Because their feet smell.
Why were the elephants banned from the swimming pool?	Because their trunks kept falling down.
Why do bees hum?	Because they don't know the words.
Why couldn't the two elephants go swimming?	Because they only had one pair of trunks.
Why can't a man's head be twelve inches wide?	Because if it was, it would be a foot.
Why can't you hang a man with a moustache?	Because you need a rope.
Why do birds fly south in winter?	Because it's too far to walk.
Why are you jumping up and down?	Because I've just taken some medicine and I forgot to shake the bottle.
Why haven't you changed the water in the goldfish bowl?	Because they haven't drunk the first lot yet.
Why are you late for work?	Because there are eight of us in our family, but the alarm clock was only set for seven.

Why do you call your baby Coffee?	Because he keeps us awake at night.
Why did the wife shoot her husband with a bow and arrow?	Because she didn't want to wake the children.
Why is it so hard to drive a golf ball?	Because it doesn't have a steering wheel.
Why did the sheep say 'Moo'?	Because it was learning a foreign language.
Why was the football team called The Scrambled Eggs?	Because they were always beaten
Why did the teacher wear sunglasses?	Because the students were so bright.
Why did the cow jump over the moon?	Because the farmer had cold hands.
Why is the letter E lazy?	Because it's always in bed.
Why did the little boy get into trouble for feeding the monkeys at the zoo?	Because he fed them to the lions.
Why do children brighten up a home?	Because they never turn off the lights.

6   BECAUSE ... 2

Why did the millionaire live in a house without a bathroom?	Because he was filthy rich.
Why did they put a fence around the graveyard?	Because people were dying to get in.
Why hasn't anyone ever stolen a canal?	Because it has too many locks.
Why is the school soccer pitch always so wet and soggy?	Because the players are always dribbling on it.
Why did the tap dancer have to retire?	Because he kept falling into the sink.
Why couldn't the sailors play cards?	Because the captain was standing on the deck.
Why did the drunk climb up on the roof?	Because he heard that drinks were on the house.
Why did the author change his name to Biro?	Because he wanted a pen name.
Why does my wife have a clean mind?	Because she changes it every few minutes.
Why did you push him under a steamroller?	Because I wanted a flat mate.

Why did he ask his mother to sit on the front step?	Because he'd always wanted a stepmother.
Why did he want to have all his teeth pulled out?	Because he wanted more gum to chew.
Why is she standing on her head?	Because she's turning things over in her mind.
Why was the Egyptian boy confused?	Because his daddy was a mummy.
Why did the boy's mother knit him three socks for his birthday.	Because he had grown another foot.
Why did the athlete blame his losing the race on his socks?	Because they were guaranteed not to run.
Why was he disqualified from the walking race?	Because he had won it two years running.
Why does you sister keep her clothes in the fridge?	Because she likes to slip into something cool in the evening.
Why did the archeologist go bankrupt?	Because his career was in ruins.
Why was the crab arrested?	Because it was always pinching things.

7 'DAFT' DEFINITIONS

Match the definitions below with a suitable word on the right. Write your answer in the boxes at the bottom of the page. Look at the example (0).

0   The only thing you can do with a ladder.

1   Someone who looks for a flat with a violin under one arm, a trombone under the other and a pet Rottweiler dog.

2   Something that keeps a person poor all his or her life so that he or she can can die rich.

3   Someone who goes into a restaurant and orders the waiter.

4   Someone who puffs on cigars, cigarettes and steps.

5   Someone who can put two and two together.

6   Someone who knows how to play ther bagpipes but doesn't.

7   Something you take when you are tired.

8   Something worn by girls.

9   A place where a guy gets stabbed in the back and instead of bleeding to death, he sings.

10 Someone who goes up to the city every day in order to make enough money to live in the country.

11 Entrance to a house.

12 A place where children go to catch colds from each other so they can stay at home.

13 Someone who travels to see things that are different and then complains when they aren't the same.

14 A car some people drive.

15 The only place where divorce comes before marriage.

a	accountant
b	address
c	adore
d	afford
e	arrest
f	cannibal
g	climate
h	commuter
i	dictionary
j	gentleman
k	life insurance
l	opera
m	optimist
n	school
o	smoker
p	tourist

0	1	2	3	4	5	6	7	8	9	10	11	12	13	14	15
g															

8 PUNS

Sort out the following puns by matching the beginnings (1–20) from column A with a suitable ending (a–t) from column B. Write your answers in the boxes at the bottom of the page.

A	**B**
1 To keep cool at a football match …	a ended up in a tie.
2 For a good birthday present for a boy, a drum …	b is just one big picnic.
3 Frogs …	c put a brick under each foot.
4 The pop group Boomerang …	d like small talk.
5 A missing Dalmatian dog …	e stand next to a fan.
6 Rubber gloves …	f tried to give his girlfriend the slip.
7 This is a new pocket-sized tape recorder for people who …	g said it was a step in the right direction.
8 The first tanning oil invented …	h thought I'd dye.
9 When high heels went out of fashion, it …	i are hoping for a comeback.
10 I know a lingerie salesman who …	j was a big let-down for many women.
11 Two silkworms were in a race. They …	k could watch time fly.
12 When I saw my hair was turning grey, I …	l are always trying to drum up business.
13 I know a jockey who …	m takes a lot of beating.
14 For most ants and wasps, life …	n could only be used on Sundays.
15 The scientist crossed a watch with an aeroplane so she …	o are usually plucky musicians.
16 My brother thinks that the headaches I get …	p come in very handy.
17 To hire a horse …	q is always horsing around.
18 When the first escalator was used, people …	r make some people jumpy.
19 Manufacturers of percussion instruments …	s are all in my mind.
20 Harpists …	t is easily spotted.

1	2	3	4	5	6	7	8	9	10	11	12	13	14	15	16	17	18	19	20

9 'CHAT UP' LINES

The man below is trying to 'chat up' different women, but without much success. Match his 'chat up' lines (1–10) with the answers he is given (a–j).

a Better than the company.
b I don't think Amanda would suit you.
c I must have been given your share.
d No, it was just bad luck.
e Nothing. I can't talk and laugh at the same time.

f OK. But mind you don't burn yourself on my cigarette!
g Why, are you falling apart?
h Why, are you leaving?
i Yes, but would you stay there?
j Yours must turn a few stomachs.

1 Do you think it was fate that brought us together?

2 Would you like to join me?

3 Your face must turn a few heads.

4 Can I kiss you?

5 What do you think of the music here?

6 I'd go to the end of the world for you.

7 Could you give me your name, please?

8 What would you say if I asked you to marry me?

9 I think I could make you very happy.

10 How did you get to be so beautiful?

10 WHO WROTE WHAT?

Try to work out who wrote the books below. Choose from the following authors.

Albert Ross	Dinah Mite	L. E. Fant	Rhoda Camel
Andrew Pictures	Gail Force	L. M. N. Tree	Robin Holmes
Andy Mann	Gladys Friday	M. T. Cupboard	Roland Butter
Anne Tarctic	Ivor Fortune	R. E. Volting	T. Shott
C. U. Later	Justin Case	R. U. Scared	Warren Peace

1 *End Of The Week* by _____

2 *How Sherlock Holmes Solved Crimes* by _____

3 *How I Crossed The Sahara Desert* by _____

4 *The Lady Artist* by _____

5 *Better Golf* by _____

6 *Flying Over The Ocean* by _____

7 *Ghost Stories* by _____

8 *Tolstoy's Greatest Novel* by _____

9 *All You Need To Know About Explosions* by _____

10 *No Food In The House* by _____

11 *Quick Breakfasts* by _____

12 *Do-It-Yourself Jobs At Home* by _____

13 *Storms And Strong Winds* by _____

14 *Confessions Of A Burglar* by _____

15 *Outsize Clothing* by _____

16 *Au Revoir* by _____

17 *The Millionaire* by _____

18 *Exploring The South Pole* by _____

19 *School Dinners* by _____

20 *The Importance Of Taking Out Insurance* by _____

11 CAR ACCIDENT CLAIMS

Whenever there is a road accident, each driver has to write a report of what happened for the insurance company. Below are some real quotations from some of these reports. Unfortunately, they are mixed up. Sort them out by matching the beginnings (1–15) from column A with a suitable ending (a–o) from column B. Write your answers in the boxes at the bottom of the page.

A	B
1 Coming home I drove into the wrong house and collided …	a was a little guy in a small car with a big mouth.
2 I thought my window was down, but I …	b make it to the other side of the road when I hit her.
3 I collided with a stationary …	c into a telephone pole.
4 A pedestrian hit me …	d ran him over.
5 He was all over the road, and I had to …	e glanced at my mother-in-law and drove into the river.
6 In an attempt to kill a fly, I drove …	f with a tree I didn't have.
7 I had been driving my car for forty years when I fell …	g bounced off the bonnet of my car.
8 My car was legally parked …	h removing my hat, found that I had fractured my skull.
9 The indirect cause of the accident …	i and went under my car.
10 The pedestrian had no idea which way to run, so I …	j hitting the bumper of the car in front, I struck the pedestrian.
11 I told the police I was not injured, but on …	k as it backed into the other vehicle.
12 I saw a slow-moving, sad-faced old gentleman as he …	l found it was up when I put my head through it.
13 I was sure the old lady would …	m swerve a number of times before I hit him.
14 To avoid …	n asleep at the wheel.
15 I pulled away from the side of the road, …	o lorry coming the other way.

1	2	3	4	5	6	7	8	9	10	11	12	13	14	15

12 WHAT ARE THEY SAYING?

Look at the pictures below and try to work out what the people are saying. Write your answer (a–j) under each drawing.

a After you!	f Excuse me, where's the police station, please?
b Bless you!	g Good luck!
c Congratulations!	h Look out!
d Do you mind if I smoke?	i Oh, sorry!
e Drive carefully!	j What's the time please?

From FUN CLASS ACTIVITIES: Book 1 by Peter Watcyn-Jones © Penguin Books 2000 PHOTOCOPIABLE

13 CARTOONS 1

Look at the cartoons below and try to work out what the missing captions (the words that go with a cartoon) are. Write your answer (a–j) under each drawing.

a	10…9…8…7…6	f	Are you sure you're not lost?
b	A room with a bath, please.	g	Hooray! A ship at last!
c	A table near the orchestra, please.	h	I just flew in from Paris.
d	Ah, you must be Emily's parents.	i	I name this child – Ouch, that hurt!
e	And this is a photo of me when I was really young.	j	What a smell! Have you been using soap again?

From FUN CLASS ACTIVITIES: Book 1 by Peter Watcyn-Jones © Penguin Books 2000 PHOTOCOPIABLE

14 CARTOONS 2

Look at the cartoons below and try to work out what the missing captions (the words that go with a cartoon) are. Write your answer (a–j) under each drawing.

a But I thought you packed the flag!

b Don't worry, It's only a light shower.

c I'm afraid you'll have to try our head office.

d It's your own fault for sunbathing!

e No, she doesn't read music. She plays by ear.

f Perhaps I'd better explain what we mean by crash course again.

g Poor Mario. He's still feeling very homesick!

h The dishwasher has broken down again.

i Well, the invitation did say 'Evening dress'.

j Would you like to pour or shall I?

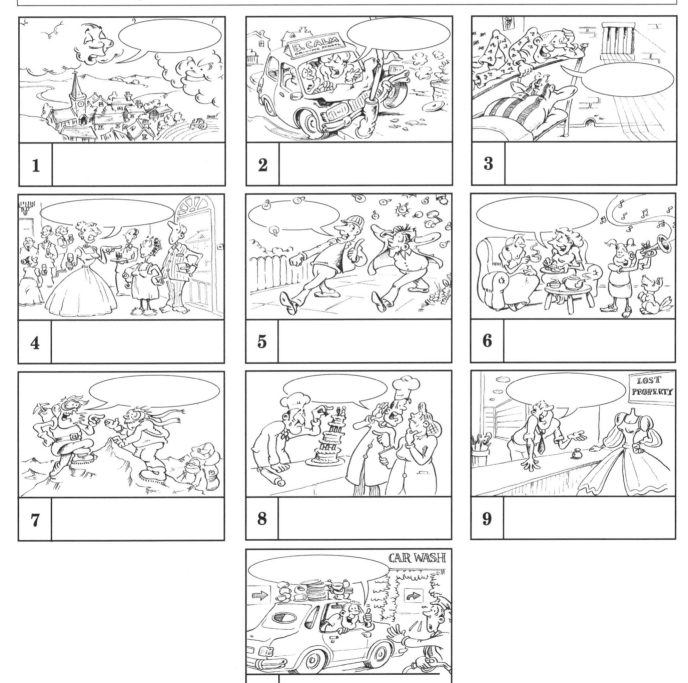

15 SIGNS

Look at the pictures below and try to work out which words are missing from each of the signs. Write your answer (a–j) under each drawing.

a BEGINNERS' MAZE
b EAR PLUGS FOR SALE
c GOING, GOING, GONE FOR LUNCH
d LIGHTNING SKETCHES
e MOTOR MECHANICS ANNUAL
   DINNER & DANCE

f ONLY A STONE'S THROW FROM
   THE BEACH
g ROWING CLUB HEADQUARTERS
h SOAP FACTORY
i TOY FACTORY
j WET PAINT

16 SORT OUT THE JOKE 1

The following joke has got mixed up. Can you sort it out? Mark each part 1–10.
Number 1 has been done for you.

could have told me that the cat was on the roof, the
next time that the cat had fallen off the roof and wasn't   _____

'The cat is just fine,' said his neighbour, 'but I   _____

neighbour to ask about his pet and the neighbour says,
'The cat has died.'   _____

think you should know that your mother's on the roof.'   _____

A man goes off on a business trip, leaving his cat with
his neighbour. A few days later he phones the   1

new cat and, a few weeks later, set off on another trip.
Once again, he left his cat with the same neighbour.   _____

The poor man is very upset and says to his friend,   _____

feeling too well, and so on.'
When he came home from his business trip he got a   _____

'Couldn't you have broken the news of my cat's
death to me more gently? The first time I phoned you   _____

After a few days he phoned and asked, 'How's the cat?'   _____

16 SORT OUT THE JOKE 1 (ALTERNATIVE)

The following joke has got mixed up. Can you sort it out? Mark each part 1–10.
Number 1 has been done for you.

The tortoise who offers to go is very worried that the
others will drink his milk shake while he is gone. But
_____

going to come back now. Let's drink his milk shake!'
_____

cafe doorway, 'If you dare touch it, I won't go for the
umbrella!'
_____

Two days pass and still he has not come back. Then
another two days. Finally, after a week, one of the
_____

Three tortoises go into a cafe and order three chocolate
<u>1</u>

'Yes, I agree!' says the second tortoise.
_____

they promise him that they won't. So he finally sets off.
_____

milk shakes. Then it starts to rain, so they decide that
one of them should go home and fetch an umbrella.
_____

Suddenly, the third tortoise shouts angrily from the
_____

tortoises who is still waiting says, 'I don't think he's
_____

17 SORT OUT THE JOKE 2

The following joke has got mixed up. Can you sort it out? Mark each part 1–11.
Number 1 has been done for you.

weeks and swing around the branches,' said the zoo's director.   _____

director explained to him that one of the zoo's major
attractions, the gorilla, had died and they needed a   _____

straight into the lion's enclosure.
When he recovered his senses he saw the lion   _____

both the sack?'   _____

The advertisement in The Stage, a 'showbiz' magazine
read: '*Non-speaking part, but you must be very athletic.*'   __1__

quite a good routine, leaping and tumbling about. And the
public seemed to love it. Indeed the crowd's applause drove   _____

substitute until the real thing could be imported.
'All you have to do is wear this gorilla suit for a few   _____

approaching and started to scream for help.
'Shut up, you fool!' said the lion. 'Do you want to get us   _____

So Jim, being out of work, applied for the job and found
himself being directed to the local Zoo. There, the zoo's   _____

him to be even more daring until one day, while attempting
a somersault he lost his grip and fell out of the tree and   _____

The few weeks turned into a month and, although it was
hot in the suit, the pay was good. Jim had even worked out   _____

From FUN CLASS ACTIVITIES: Book 1 by Peter Watcyn-Jones © Penguin Books 2000 PHOTOCOPIABLE

18 SORT OUT THE JOKE 3

The following joke has got mixed up. Can you sort it out? Mark each part 1–11. Number 1 has been done for you.

of 'Ham sandwiches, I can't bear them any more!' he ran along the roof of the building and flung himself off, falling ten floors to his death.
The Scotsman then opened his lunch box, found salmon   _____

prospect of Irish cheddar sandwiches yet again, he leapt off the roof to his death.
At the funeral for the three men, held a week later, the three   _____

An Englishman, a Scotsman and an Irishman were all working on the same building site together, and they always stopped at 1

sniffed loudly, 'I just don't understand Paddy's behaviour at all – he always made his own sandwiches!'   _____

sandwiches and screamed, 'Och no, salmon again. I can't bear it any more!' and in turn flung himself off the building to his death.
Finally, the Irishman opened his lunch box and, faced with the   _____

screamed, 'Oh, no, not ham sandwiches again. If I have ham sandwiches again, I'm seriously going to kill myself.'
The Scotsman opened his lunch box and, like the Englishman screamed, 'Och no – salmon sandwiches again. If the wife   _____

sobbed, 'I don't understand it either. Jock would have said something if he really didn't like salmon.' Finally the Irish wife   _____

makes me these one more time, I'm going to kill myself.'
The Irishman then opened his lunch box and exclaimed loudly, 'Holy Mother of God! If I have cheese sandwiches once more, I   _____

widows were weeping together. The English wife said, 'I don't understand. I thought he liked ham.' The Scotsman's widow   _____

tell you, I'm going to kill myself.'
Next day, lunchtime came round again. The Englishman opened his sandwiches only to find ham again. With a loud cry   _____

the same time to eat their packed lunches. One day the Englishman opened up his plastic lunch container and   _____

From FUN CLASS ACTIVITIES: Book 1 by Peter Watcyn-Jones © Penguin Books 2000 PHOTOCOPIABLE

Working together, sort out the joke. You can read the sentences to your partner, but you mustn't show them to him/her. Mark the parts 1–10. You have parts 1, 3, 5, 7, and 9.

'Not every day, now. Do you know what I mean?

☐

Old Jake was feeling ill, so he went to see the doctor.

1

'Dead!' said the doctor. 'But how? Was it the medicine? Was it too strong?'

☐

'This is very strong stuff,' said the doctor. 'Don't take it every day, Jake.'

☐

A month later, the doctor saw Jake's wife in the street and asked how her husband was.

☐

---

19 SORT OUT THE JOKE 4

STUDENT B

Working together, sort out the joke. You can read the sentences to your partner, but you mustn't show them to him/her. Mark the parts 1–10. You have parts 2, 4, 6, 8 and 10.

'Oh, he's dead,' she said.

☐

The doctor wanted to make sure old Jake understood, so he said once again,

☐

'No, the medicine wasn't that strong,' she said. 'It was all that skipping!'

☐

The doctor gave him a bottle of medicine.

☐

'Take it tomorrow, then skip a day, then take it the next day and skip another day, and so on.'

☐

Working together, sort out the joke. You can read the sentences to your partner, but you mustn't show them to him/her. Mark the parts 1–12. You have parts 1, 3, 5, 7, 9 and 11.

When they arrived at the police station, Manners waited outside on the steps while Shut-up went in. ☐

'Sitting outside on the steps,' replied Shut-up. ☐

Three boys called Manners, Shut-up and Trouble were playing in the woods one day, when Trouble suddenly 1

'Are your looking for trouble?' he said. ☐

'Shut-up,' replied the boy. ☐

him. They ran and shouted and ran and shouted, but Trouble had managed to get himself totally lost. So ☐

Working together, sort out the joke. You can read the sentences to your partner, but you mustn't show them to him/her. Mark the parts 1–12. You have parts 2, 4, 6, 8, 10 and 12.

Shut-up and Manners decide to go and report Trouble's disappearance to the police. ☐

'Eh?' said the policeman, startled. 'Where's your manners?' ☐

'Yes,' said Shut-up. 'How did you know?' ☐

The policeman started to get angry. ☐

vanished from sight! Although they looked everywhere, Shut-up and Manners were unable to find ☐

'What's your name, son?' asked the policeman behind the enquiry desk. ☐

21 SORT OUT THE JOKES 1

Below are two jokes that have got mixed up. Can you sort them out? Mark joke 1 A1–A6 and joke 2 B1–B7. (The first part of each joke has been done for you.)

'Lord save me! Lord save me! Amen!'
And of course the camel stopped – right on the very

_____

half-way through a joke-telling session.
'89!' said the first prisoner and the other three
giggled hysterically.

_____

'42!' he tried again. Silence.
He turned to one of his cell mates and asked what he
was doing wrong.

_____

A man buying a camel was advised that to make it
walk he should say 'Few!', to make it run he should say

A1

Four prisoners, who had shared a cell for so long, knew
each other's jokes so well that they gave them all

B1

'Many!' he shouted, and the camel began to run
– straight for the edge of a cliff. But the new owner had

_____

numbers rather than tell them.
One day a new prisoner was put in the same cell

_____

'It's not the jokes,' he was told. 'It's the way you
tell them!'

_____

forgotten the word to make the camel stop. As the cliff
edge came closer and closer he called out in terror:

_____

the cell floor.
The new inmate thought he would have a go.
'66!' he said. There was silence.

_____

edge of the precipice. Whereupon the rider wiped his
brow in relief and said, 'Phew, that was clo–AAAGH!'

_____

'96!' shouted the second and there were hoots of
laughter from the other three.
'192!' cried the third and the four rolled round

_____

'Many!' and to make it stop he should say 'Amen!'
At his first ride all went well.
'Few!' he called, and off the camel went.

_____

Below are three jokes that have got mixed up. Can you sort them out? Mark joke 1 A1–A5, joke 2 B1–B6 and joke 3 C1–C5. The first part of each joke has been done for you.

( )

the car reached 70 kilometres per hour, the chicken passed it and turned down a dirt road. It was then that the man noticed that the chicken had three legs.

( )

12,224 head.'
The man looked surprised.
'Amazing!' he cried. 'I'm the owner of that

( ) he wanted – a beautiful African bird – and decided to bid for it. The bidding went higher and higher, but finally the man

( ) 'Yep,' replied the farmer. 'Most people like drumsticks, so we developed this breed.' 'How do they taste?' asked Henry.

( )

the most important question about the parrot. 'Does the parrot talk?' he asked the auctioneer anxiously.

A fast train raced along the border of the biggest cattle ranch in Texas. A passenger gazed at the huge herds and

 Driving along a country road, Henry noticed a chicken running alongside his car. He increased his speed to 50 kilometres

(C1) A man who wanted to buy a parrot went to an animal auction. He found just what

He followed it to a farm that was filled with three-legged chickens.
'Say,' said Henry to the farmer, 'do all your chickens have three legs?

'Of course he talks,' replied the auctioneer. 'Who do you think was bidding against you?'

when the other boundary of the ranch was reached he turned to the man beside him and said:
'What a big herd of cattle! I counted

per hour.
The chicken kept coming. Henry put his foot down on the accelerator, but the chicken still managed to keep up. When

'Nothing to it. I just counted their legs and divided by four!'

'Don't rightly know,' answered the farmer. 'Haven't been able to catch one yet!'

was the winning bidder. He went excitedly to collect his bird and suddenly remembered that he had forgotten to ask

ranch and I know you're exactly right. There really are 12,224 head of cattle. How did you manage to count them when we were speeding so fast?

23 SORT OUT THE JOKES 3　　　STUDENT A

Working together, sort out the three jokes. You can read your parts of the jokes out, but you mustn't show them to anyone else in the group. Mark the first joke 1–5, the second 6–10 and the third 11–16. You have the first part of joke 1.

An Englishman went to Ireland to do a spot of fishing. He found a suitable spot by a river and prepared to wade out into the murky water with his

☐ 1

reds, a yellow and a brown.'
'And what do you eat for lunch?'
'For lunch? Two pinks, a red and a blue.'

☐

road and bumped straight into a farmer who was driving some more cows into a field. He stood and listened while the motorist told him the amazing

☐

'You said it was shallow!' he cried as he made his way back to the river bank completely soaked.

☐

---

23 SORT OUT THE JOKES 3　　　STUDENT B

Working together, sort out the three jokes. You can read your parts of the jokes out, but you mustn't show them to anyone else in the group. Mark the first joke 1–5, the second 6–10 and the third 11–16. You have the first part of joke 2.

A sportsman – a snooker player – went to the doctor saying he thought his diet wasn't healthy enough and was making him ill.

☐ 6

hard look under the bonnet, then said, 'It's the battery that's the problem.'
The motorist was so stunned that he ran down the

☐

wellingtons. But before he did so he asked a farmer who was mending a nearby fence if the water was shallow.

☐

'And for tea?'
'Oh, for tea a black and three reds.'
'I see,' said the doctor. 'Well, it's obvious

☐

From FUN CLASS ACTIVITIES: Book 1 by Peter Watcyn-Jones © Penguin Books 2000 PHOTOCOPIABLE

23 SORT OUT THE JOKE 3

STUDENT C

Working together, sort out the three jokes. You can read your parts of the jokes out, but you mustn't show them to anyone else in the group. Mark the first joke 1–5, the second 6–10 and the third 11–16.

'Sure, the water's shallow,' came the reply.
With this the angler walked straight in to the river –
and found himself up to his neck.

☐

story of what had happened.
'Was she a white cow with a brown patch
between her eyes?' the farmer asked.

☐

'Well, I thought it was,' said the farmer. 'It
only comes up to the waists of the ducks, and
they're only twenty centimetres tall.'

☐

said the farmer. 'That's Daisy and she doesn't
know a thing about cars!'

☐

---

23 SORT OUT THE JOKES 3

STUDENT D

Working together, sort out the three jokes. You can read your parts of the jokes out, but you mustn't show them to anyone else in the group. Mark the first joke 1–5, the second 6–10 and the third 11–16. You have the first part of joke 3.

A motorist who had broken down on a country
road was staring hopelessly into the engine when
a cow came along. To his surprise, it took a long

☐ 11

what the matter is.'
'What is it?' asked the sportsman.
'You're not getting enough greens!'

☐

'Yes! Yes, that's right!' cried the motorist.
'I wouldn't take any notice if I were you,'

☐

'What do you eat in the mornings?' asked
the doctor.
'Snooker balls,' said the sportsman. 'Two

☐

24 SORT OUT THE PUNCH LINES 1

In the following 12 jokes, the punch lines (in bold) have got mixed up. See if you can work out which punch line belongs to which joke. Write your answers in the boxes at the bottom of the page. Number 1 has been done for you.

Joke 1
Sam: Have you got holes in your socks?
Katie: Certainly not.
Sam: **Well, I didn't.**

Joke 2
An Englishman, a Scotsman and an Irishman went for a walk in the country.
Englishman: Look at that beautiful English cow!
Irishman: It looks more like an Irish cow to me.
Scotsman: You're both wrong. It's a Scottish cow. **It will be miles away by now!**

Joke 3
Young Jimmy: Dad, did you know there's a black cat in the dining room?
Father: Don't worry, Jimmy. Black cats are very lucky.
Young Jimmy: Well this one certainly is. **I'm a boxer.**

Joke 4
A policeman sees a man trying to cross the road at a very dangerous place. The man has been trying to cross for about five minutes.
Policeman: Excuse me, sir, there's a zebra crossing only fifty metres away.
Man: **Then how do you get your feet in?**

Joke 5
Jennifer: I went on a Chinese diet once.
Helen: Chinese diet? What's that?
Jennifer: **It's eating your dinner!**

Joke 6
Child: A bee stung me on the nose.
Teacher: I'll put cream on it.
Child: It's too late. **Look, it's got bagpipes!**

Joke 7
Brian: You need to be a very good singer in our house.
Alan: Oh? Why's that?
Brian: **They only give you one chopstick!**

Joke 8
Tourist: Good evening. I wonder if I could stay here for the night?
Farmer: All right. But you'll have to make your own bed.
Tourist: Oh, that's all right.
Farmer: **Okay. In that case I'll have two.**

Joke 9
Susan: How did you break your leg?
Tom: See that hole over there?
Susan: Yes.
Tom: **There's no lock on the bathroom door.**

Joke 10
Claire: Do you believe in free speech?
Mandy: Yes, of course.
Claire: Good. **Here's some wood and a hammer.**

Joke 11
Optician: Here are your new glasses, sir. But only wear them when you work.
Man: Oh, that could be difficult.
Optician: Why's that?
Man: **Well, I hope it's having better luck than I am!**

Joke 12
Salesman: This machine will cut your work in half.
Customer: **Can I use your telephone?**

1	2	3	4	5	6	7	8	9	10	11	12
4											

25 SORT OUT THE PUNCH LINES 2

In the following 12 jokes, the punch lines (in bold) have got mixed up. See if you can work out which punch line belongs to which joke. Write your answers in the boxes at the bottom of the page.

Joke 1
Man: What are you going to do with that pile of manure?
Farmer: Put it on my strawberries.
Man: **That was the echo!**

Joke 2
Aunt Mary: Now tell me, Jenny, what will you do when you are as big as your mother?
Five-year-old Jenny: **You're talking rubbish again!**

Joke 3
Kath: Whenever I see a mirror I can never resist looking into it for at least a few minutes to admire my perfect complexion. Do you think that's vanity?
Samantha: No. **Who's winning?**

Joke 4
Harry: Why are you walking like a crab?
Bob: It's these new pills I'm taking. **But it's got no atmosphere.**

Joke 5
Steve: What's high, pointed and has ears?
Julie: I don't know. What?
Steve: A mountain.
Julie: But what about the ears?
Steve: **I always put cream on mine.**

Joke 6
1st man (at concert): What's that book the conductor is looking at.
2nd man: That's the score.
1st man: Really? **We just missed it!**

Joke 7
Wife: There's a man out there wringing his hands.
Husband: I'm not surprised. **More like imagination.**

Joke 8
Kevin: First I had appendicitis, then thrombosis, then tonsillitis. Next came amnesia, and I thought I was finished when they gave me vaccination and inoculation.
Clive: How awful!
Kevin: Yes, wasn't it? **Haven't you ever heard of mountaineers?**

Joke 9
American tourist: Excuse me, when was the Magna Carta signed?'
Guide: 1215, madam.
American tourist (looking at her watch): What a pity! **The bell doesn't work.**

Joke 10
Pupil: Sir! Empty Coke cans, fish-and-chip paper, paper bags, used tissues, broken bottles, empty cardboard boxes …
Teacher: Robert! **Go on a diet.**

Joke 11
Dentist: Good grief! You've got the biggest cavity I've ever seen … the biggest cavity I've ever seen.
Patient: You don't have to repeat yourself!
Dentist: I didn't. **They have side effects.**

Joke 12
These astronauts went to the moon. And the first thing they saw when they came out of their spaceship was a Chinese restaurant.
1st astronaut: Would you believe it, there's a Chinese restaurant on the moon.
2nd astronaut: Yes. **I thought that spelling test would never end!**

1	2	3	4	5	6	7	8	9	10	11	12

26 SORT OUT THE PUNCH LINES 3

In the following jokes, the words in the last line (the punch line) have got mixed up. Try to sort them out and write down the correct version.

Joke 1

Tramp: Excuse me, lady, you wouldn't give me 30p for a bun, would you?
Woman: I don't know. _____

(to first. at I the want bun look)

Joke 2

We came across a Cherokee tribe. The chief greeted me. He said, 'How!'
And I said, 'How!'
Then he said, 'How!'
And I said, 'How!'
'Hey, Frank, I didn't know you could speak Cherokee.'
'_____ ,

(when how. It's know easy you)

Joke 3

Man: Will the band play anything I request?
Waiter: Certainly, sir.
Man: _____

(them play tell cards. to Then)

Joke 4

Mother (angrily): Nigel! Why did you fall in that mud wearing your new trousers?
Nigel: _____

(to there off! Because them time take wasn't)

Joke 5

An American visitor to Britain was a passenger in a train. After a while he got into conversation with an Englishman sitting opposite.
American: Do you know that you can board a train in Texas, and after travelling for 24 hours you'd still be in Texas.
Englishman: Yes, I know. _____

(trains country. that We this too. have in like)

Joke 6

Mother: How did you get that swelling on your nose?
Child: I bent down to smell a brose.
Mother: It's not brose, it's rose. There's no *b* in rose.
Child: _____

(this There in one! was)

Joke 7

Fred: What's that piece of string tied around your finger for?
Bob: My mother put it there to remind me to post a letter for her.
Fred: And did you post it?
Bob: _____

(forgot to give No. it me. She to)

Joke 8

Tom: I've just bought a pig.
Emma: Where are you going to keep it?
Tom: Under my bed.
Emma: But what about the smell?
Tom: _____

(that. Oh, mind the won't pig)

Joke 9

Child: Mum, remember that special plate you were always so worried I would break?
Mother: Yes, why?
Child: _____

(are your over. Well, worries)

Joke 10

Singer: Do you like music?
Audience member: Yes. _____

_____

(finish were song But singing. you please the)

From FUN CLASS ACTIVITIES: Book 1 by Peter Watcyn-Jones © Penguin Books 2000 PHOTOCOPIABLE

In the following jokes, the words in the last line (the punch line) have got mixed up. Try to sort them out and write down the correct version.

Joke 1

Colin: In China I saw a woman hanging from a tree.
Pam: Shanghai?
Colin: _____

(feet a ground. No, few the just off)

Joke 2

Passenger: Single to Manchester, please.
Clerk: That'll be nine pounds fifty. Change at Crewe.
Passenger: _____

_____

(change mind. you my here, don't I'll if have)

Joke 3

Two men were sitting on the bank of a river in Africa, dangling their feet in the water. Suddenly, one let out a yell and the other said, 'What's the matter?'
'A crocodile has just bitten off one of my feet.'
'Which one?'
'How would I know?' came the reply. '_____

_____ ,

(same look Those the to crocodiles me. all)

Joke 4

Best-selling author: It seemed to me, after fifteen years of full-time writing, that I was absolutely hopeless and had no talent at all for writing.'
Interviewer: So what did you do? Decide to give up writing?
Author: Oh, no! _____

(time famous. was By I far that too)

Joke 5

1st woman: Every week my aunts and uncles and cousins come over and we all sit around and make sweaters.
2nd woman: That's nice.
1st woman: _____

(closely Yes, family. a we're very knit)

Joke 6

1st man: When you're losing your hair at the front, it means you're a great thinker. And when you're losing your hair at the back, it means you're a great lover.
2nd man: But I'm losing my hair at the front and the back!
1st man: _____

(you lover! you're That great means think a)

Joke 7

Susan: Can you spell 'blind bird'?
Mandy: Yes. B-L-I-N-D B-I-R-D.
Susan: Wrong. It's B-L-N-D B-R-D. _____

_____

(two it blind. had wouldn't If I's be it)

Joke 8

Son: Dad, where was I born?
Father: In London.
Son: Where were you born?
Father: In Sydney.
Son: And where was Mum born?
Father: In Copenhagen.
Son: _____

(up! all that met it we amazing Isn't)

Joke 9

A man goes to visit his friend in hospital. His friend is covered from head to foot in bandages.
Man: What happened?
Friend: I went through a plate glass window.
Man: _____

(wearing you those were Good bandages! thing)

Joke 10

A Scotsman was going across the Forth Bridge on a train and he hadn't bought a ticket. The inspector refused to believe that he'd lost it, but the Scotsman stuck to his story. Eventually the inspector lost his temper, picked up the Scotsman's suitcase and threw it into the water below.
'Oh, come on,' said the Scotsman. '_____

_____ ,

(believe murder don't brother! no my Just me, to because wee there's you need)

28 SORT OUT THE CAPTIONS 1

Look at the cartoons below. The wrong captions have been printed under each of them. Try to work out which caption goes with which cartoon. Write your answers in the boxes at the bottom of the page.

1	No idea. Must be a foreign language.
2	Good morning, Janet. Enjoy the skiing holiday?
3	There's someone here with a bunch of flowers for you, Simon.
4	This job really makes me sick sometimes!
5	I've dried the dishes, Mum. What shall I do next?
6	How many times have I told you not to smoke in bed!
7	I wish you wouldn't bring your work home with you, Alan.
8	I think your dad likes his birthday present.
9	Been fishing here long?

| 10 | Hello, hello, hello! |

1	2	3	4	5	6	7	8	9	10

From FUN CLASS ACTIVITIES: Book 1 by Peter Watcyn-Jones © Penguin Books 2000 *PHOTOCOPIABLE*

29 SORT OUT THE CAPTIONS 2

Look at the cartoons below. The wrong captions have been printed under each of them. Try to work out which caption goes with which cartoon. Write your answers in the boxes at the bottom of the page.

1 That must be the new sweeper Manchester United have got.

2 Must go now. I've got a train to catch.

3 Darling, do you think the central heating's up too high?

4 Well, it did say for best results use at least three coats.

5 Will you hold my hand?

6 You haven't broken down again, have you?

7 Would you like breakfast in bed today?

8 For some reason I seem to bring out the worst in people.

9 She has problems reaching the high notes.

10 He's very good at bird impressions!

1	2	3	4	5	6	7	8	9	10

From FUN CLASS ACTIVITIES: Book 1 by Peter Watcyn-Jones © Penguin Books 2000 PHOTOCOPIABLE

Work with a partner. You both have a story called 'The Bird'. But your versions are not the same. There are at least 10 differences.

Take it in turns to ask and answer questions to try to find what is different. Put a circle around any differences you find. (But don't tell your partner!)

You can ask, e.g.

What is my friend called?
Who did his grandmother call in?
Where did she live?
etc.

(NOTE: Only answer the questions your partner asks. Do not give him/her any extra information!)

The Bird

My friend David's grandmother called in some gas-fitters to fix a faulty and rather old gas fire in her house in Manchester. At 10 o'clock in the morning on the day in question, a Saturday, two men turned up and set about fixing the fire. Gran decided to go into town and do some shopping while they were doing this.

The gas-fitters were not very efficient. They kept on dropping their tools and even smashed one of the tiles on the fireplace. After forty-five minutes or so, there were bits of the fire all over the room. What's more, the gas fire was leaking quite a bit while they were taking it apart. Eventually though, they finally managed to get it back together again. It was nearly 11.30.

As they stood up to have a cigarette, one of them noticed that the lady's pet budgie had fallen off its perch and was lying on the floor of its cage with its little legs in the air. They went over to the cage. The budgie was stone dead! They realised that the old lady wouldn't be very pleased when she came home and saw that they had gassed her pet. So the two men took some copper wire and fastened the dead bird upright on its perch. Anyone coming in now would think the bird was alive and well. Then they cleared up. They had just finished when they heard the front door opening. The old lady had returned.

A few minutes later, she came into the living-room. She looked first at the fireplace and then at the budgie cage in the corner. Her face went pale, she let out a loud scream and fainted!

When the two men had revived her, she explained that she had been deeply shocked to see the budgie on its perch again – as it had died earlier that morning.

(Adapted from: Urban Myths by Phil Healey and Rick Glanvill, Virgin Books 1992).

When you have finished, compare your texts. Who found the most differences?

Work with a partner. You both have a story called 'The Bird'. But your versions are not the same. There are at least 10 differences.

Take it in turns to ask and answer questions to try to find what is different. Put a circle around any differences you find. (But don't tell your partner!)

You can ask, e.g.

What is my friend called?
What was faulty?
What time did the two men arrive?
etc.

(NOTE: Only answer the questions your partner asks. Do not give him/her any extra information!)

The Bird

My friend David's auntie called in some gas-fitters to fix a faulty and rather old-fashioned gas fire in her flat in Manchester. At 11 o'clock in the morning on the day in question, a Friday, two men turned up and set about fixing the fire. The aunt decided to go into town and visit the library while they were doing this.

The gas-fitters were not very intelligent. They kept on dropping their tools and even smashed one of the ornaments on the mantelpiece. After fifty-five minutes or so, there were bits of the fire all over the room. What's more, the gas fire was leaking quite a bit while they were repairing it. Eventually though, they finally managed to get it back together again. It was nearly 11.40.

As they stood up to have a cup of tea, one of them noticed that the lady's pet budgie had fallen off its perch and was lying on the floor of its cage with one of its little legs in the air. They went over to the cage. The budgie was stone dead! They realised that the old lady wouldn't be very happy when she came home and saw that they had poisoned her pet. So the two men took some string and tied the dead bird upright on its perch. Anyone coming in now would think the bird was alive and well. Then they cleared up. They had just finished when they heard a car pulling up outside. The old lady had returned.

Ten minutes later, she came into the lounge. She looked first at the two men and then at the budgie cage near the window. Her face went bright red, she let out a loud scream and fainted!

When the two men had revived her, she explained that she had been amazed to see the budgie on its perch again – as it had died during the night.

(Adapted from: Urban Myths by Phil Healey and Rick Glanvill, Virgin Books 1992).

When you have finished, compare your texts. Who found the most differences?

31 CARTOON STRIP

Look at the cartoon strip below. The words under the drawings are in the wrong places. Can you sort them out? Which words go with which drawing? Write your answers here:

Drawing	Correct Words	Drawing	Correct Words	Drawing	Correct Words
1	————	4	————	7	————
2	————	5	————	8	————
3	————	6	————		

The man at the bus stop

1 So the man picked up the dog...	**2** 'No, that's very kind of you,' replied the lady.
3 A man was waiting at a bus stop eating a hamburger and chips.	**4** 'Do you mind if I throw him a bit?' asked the man.
5 ...and threw him across the road.	**6** A lady with a dog came up and stood beside him, also waiting for the bus.
7 It jumped up on the man trying to get at the food.	**8** The dog smelled the food and got very excited.

32 RIGHT WORD – WRONG PLACE

One or two words in each of the jokes below are in the wrong places. Try to sort out which words are wrong and where they should be instead. Write your answers (on a separate piece of paper) like this:

Joke No.	Wrong word	Correct word	Joke No
1	stealing	missing	7
	etc.		

(NOTE: There are 10 pairs of words to be found altogether.)

Joke 1 *(2 words wrong)*

Centre-forward: I could kick myself for **stealing** that goal.
Football Coach: Don't bother. You'd recently miss.

Joke 2 *(1 word wrong)*

Father: Who's that at the door?
Son: A man with a number.
Father: Tell him to beat it.

Joke 3 *(2 words wrong)*

The bank director was distressed by the young trainee's facility with outlaws. He said, 'Where did you learn your maths?'
And the trainee said, 'Yale.'
'Yale. And what's your name?'
'Yerry Yackson.'

Joke 4 *(1 word wrong)*

A man driving an old wreck of a car drove up to the toll bridge.
'£5,' said the toll collector.
'Sold!' said the cannibal.

Joke 5 *(2 words wrong)*

The dog entered the bar, sat up on a stool and ordered a gin and tonic. The barman served him. The dog approached him, swallowed the drink, put some money on the bar and left.
'That's real,' said a drinker who had watched the whole thing.
'Yes,' said the barman. 'He usually has a whisky.'

Joke 6 *(2 words wrong)*

The little boy in the crowded department store was obviously impressed. 'I've lost my dad,' he sobbed when the policeman thanked him.
'What's your dad like?' said the policeman.
'Beer, football and the odd bet,' said the lad.

Joke 7 *(2 words wrong)*

A man was leaning on the bar enjoying a pint when one of his mates yelled, 'Hey, Pete, there's some bloke missing your car!'
Pete dashed from the pub but came back five minutes later all puffed out.
'Did you get him?' pressed his mates.
'No, ' puffed Pete. 'But it's okay. I took his drum.'

Joke 8 *(2 words wrong)*

Mary went into a pet shop.
'How much are the tourists?' she asked.
'£8 apiece.'
'But I'd like a broken one!'

Joke 9 *(1 word wrong)*

Did you hear about the driver who went on a sea voyage? When he sat down for dinner on the first night out he sent back the menu and asked for the passenger list.

Joke 10 *(2 words wrong)*

LOST DOG: Has three legs, blind in left eye, large scar on throat, right ear missing, tail whole in two places, no teeth, probably castrated. Answers to Lucky.

Joke 11 *(1 word wrong)*

Holidaymaker: What's your pig's name?
Farmer: Ballpoint.
Holidaymaker: Is that his amazing name?
Farmer: No, it's his pen name.

Joke 12 *(2 words wrong)*

The guide was showing American kittens around London. He said, 'On this spot here was the famous Tyburn Tree where so many figures were hung.'
An American said, 'Did they hang people often?'
The guide said, 'No, I don't think so. Once was usually enough.'

33 MISPRINTS 1

Sometimes what you read in a newspaper is not exactly what the newspaper intended. A letter in the wrong place or left out can completely change the meaning of a sentence. Work in pairs. Look at the following extracts from newspapers and magazines. Each contains a misprint. Write down which word is wrong and then suggest which word should have been used instead. Look at the example (0).

0   Jewellery worth over £1,500 has been stolen from a mouse in Birmingham.

1   His first book, *Beekeeping for Beginners,* was a great success and made him a lot of honey.

2   He won Wimbledon by eating Pete Sampras in the final.

3   The children's party was hell on Saturday at St. Joseph's church.

4   The winners of the holiday competition will receive free fights, hotel rooms, all meals and £500 spending money.

5   WANTED: Single woman to share fat with two others. Central London.

6   The fire brigade were called in to rescue a car which was stuck on top of the library roof.

7   One of the soldiers dropped his gin while they were marching past the Queen.

8   The police are looking for a man with a long, black bear.

9   To get a loan you must sing this form.

10 God for sale. Black Labrador. 1 year old.

11 She has been working at the Ministry for Defence for seven years, mainly cleaning officers there.

12 Beethoven was unable to hear his Ninth Symphony because by that time he was completely dead.

13 He gave his girlfriend a red nose on St. Valentine's Day.

14 Crows gathered at Heathrow to greet the arrival of Michael Jackson.

15 Window, aged 50, good sense of humour, seeks mature man for friendship, possibly marriage.

Write your answers here.

	Wrong word	Correct word		Wrong word	Correct word
0	mouse	house	8		
1			9		
2			10		
3			11		
4			12		
5			13		
6			14		
7			15		

34 MISPRINTS 2

Sometimes what you read in a newspaper is not exactly what the newspaper intended. A letter in the wrong place or left out can completely change the meaning of a sentence. Work in pairs. Look at the following extracts from newspapers and magazines. Each contains a misprint. Write down which word is wrong and then suggest which word should have been used instead. Look at the example (0).

0   For Sale: Gent's skirt, 16-inch collar.

1   Queen Victoria was on the thorn for 63 years.

2   Jenny was late for school today because she missed her bust.

3   Earlier the same afternoon, Mrs Wilkins slipped off a bus and bruised a ship.

4   Due to repairs to the air-conditioning system, offices will be very humid for the next three days. Please bare with us.

5   FOR RENT: Fully furnished house. Includes three toilets. £200 per wee.

6   3–course meal. £15. Price includes wind and coffee.

7   He received his degree in unclear physics.

8   A secret ballet was held to elect a new chairperson.

9   It is said that there are more golf curses per square mile in North Carolina than anywhere in the world.

10 FOUND: One white rabbi with brown ears.

11 Superintendent James said that more polite dogs were to be used to help control crowds at football matches.

12 Playboy Enterprises estimates that removing ornamental pants from its offices will save $27,000 a year.

13 EXTERMINATING: We are trained to kill all pets.

14 The doctor felt her patient's purse.

15 To clean your oven, put ammonia and water in a pan and sit in the oven.

Write your answers here.

	Wrong word	Correct word		Wrong word	Correct word
0	skirt	shirt	8		
1			9		
2			10		
3			11		
4			12		
5			13		
6			14		
7			15		

35 MISPRINTS 3

Sometimes what you read in a newspaper is not exactly what the newspaper intended. A letter in the wrong place or left out can completely change the meaning of a sentence. Work in pairs. Look at the following extracts from newspapers and magazines. Each contains a misprint. Write down which word is wrong and then suggest which word should have been used instead. Look at the example (0).

0   Special this week: meal plus bottle of wind for only £6.

1   The restaurant served a wide range of inexpensive, nasty snacks.

2   Apart from her host and hostess, everyone else at the party was a strangler.

3   John Collins has been a pretty officer on the QE2 for over five years.

4   Today's talk will be given by General McKenzie – a battle-scared veteran of two world wars.

5   The announcement that the vicar had raided a fund for the support of the unfortunate man's wife will be welcomed by all.

6   The best treatment for shock is to rape the patient in a blanket.

7   I only hope people will come along in peace tonight and enjoy a good fight.

8   Au pair wanted: peasant working conditions.

9   Mr Brown, a 66-year-old pensioner, showed great courage in tickling the two youths who tried to steal his car.

10 There were scenes of disorder in the House of Commons last night, with one member of the Opposition shaking a fish at the Prime Minister.

11 Ice-cream sellers in London say they have ordered huge socks because of the unusually hot weather.

12 Free bottle of wine for the first twenty people who die at our restaurant on Saturday evening.

13 My uncle is a defective Inspector in the South Wales police force.

14 Politicians are worried about the treat of another war in the Middle East.

15 Mobile beautician requires assistant. Good salary plus free scar.

Write your answers here.

	Wrong word	Correct word		Wrong word	Correct word
0	wind	wine	8		
1			9		
2			10		
3			11		
4			12		
5			13		
6			14		
7			15		

From FUN CLASS ACTIVITIES: Book 1 by Peter Watcyn-Jones © Penguin Books 2000 PHOTOCOPIABLE

The following newspaper extracts, headlines, etc. are written in such a way that there is an extra unexpected meaning to the one that was intended – often with amusing results! Take it in turns to try to explain the 'other' meaning.

1 It is bad manners to break your bread and roll in your soup.

2 The chairman spoke briefly, much to the delight of the audience.

3 CANCER LINKED TO SMOKING IN A STUDY

4 Dinner special: Turkey £6, Chicken or Beef £5; Children £3.50.

5 A man who almost strangled his ex-wife was given a second chance by the judge.

6 FENCING IN YOUR SWIMMING POOL CAN SAVE A CHILD'S LIFE

7 Tired of cleaning yourself? Let me do it.

8 Wanted: Man to take care of cow that does not smoke or drink.

9 The ladies of the Helping Hand Society enjoyed a swap social on Friday evening. Everybody brought something they didn't need. Many of the ladies were accompanied by their husbands.

10 Our bikinis are exciting and different. They are simply the tops!

11 POLICE DISCOVER CRACK IN AUSTRALIA

12 THUGS EAT THEN ROB RESTAURANT OWNER

13 DEALERS WILL HEAR CAR TALK FRIDAY NOON

14 TWO SISTERS REUNITED AFTER 18 YEARS IN CHECKOUT QUEUE

15 CALF BORN TO FARMER WITH TWO HEADS

16 She died in the home in which she was born at the age of 88.

17 CEMETERY ALLOWS PEOPLE TO BE BURIED BY THEIR PETS

18 We saw many bears driving through Yellowstone Park.

19 FOR SALE: Bulldog. Will eat anything. Loves children.

20 Yoko Ono will talk about her husband, John Lennon, who was killed in an interview with Barbara Walters.

The following newspaper extracts, headlines, etc. are written in such a way that there is an extra unexpected meaning to the one that was intended – often with amusing results! Take it in turns to try to explain the 'other' meaning.

1 The death of the Prime Minister was the turning point in his life.

2 FOR SALE: a baby's high chair that can be made into a table, pushchair, potty, rocking horse, vacuum cleaner, fur coat and Elvis Presley CD.

3 The bride was wearing an old lace gown that fell to the floor as she walked down the aisle.

4 Migraines strike twice as many women as do men.

5 MILK DRINKERS ARE TURNING TO POWDER

6 Two cars were reported stolen by the Surrey police yesterday.

7 The patient was referred to a psychiatrist with a severe emotional problem.

8 A 30-year-old Copenhagen man was found murdered by his parents in his home late last night.

9 KICKING BABY CONSIDERED TO BE HEALTHY

10 That summer I finally got my leg operated on. What a relief! It had been hanging over my head for years.

11 An oil spill was first reported to the Coast Guard by a man who saw oil covered rocks walking along the shore.

12 He ran outside and chased after the burglar with a baseball bat in his underwear.

13 Delightful country cottage, 2 bedrooms, large lounge, kitchen, bathroom, coloured suite, toilet 5 miles from Epsom.

14 UNEMPLOYED man seeks work. Completely honest and trustworthy, will take anything.

15 1929 Rolls-Royce hearse for sale. Original body.

16 LENIN'S BODY MOVED

17 I have just heard that we do have film of the astronaut's breakfast, which should be coming up shortly.

18 She has visited the cemetery where her husband was buried on a number of occasions.

19 NEW YORK BAN ON BOXING AFTER DEATH

20 TOILETS OUT OF ORDER, please use platforms 7–8.

38 STRANGE BUT TRUE!

Fill in the missing words in the sentences below. Choose from the following. Not all the words will be used.

verbs		nouns		adjectives
eat	repair	bullet	leaflets	biggest
feel	requires	corpse	nose	black and white
invented	studied	grapes	photo	blue
needs	take place	handbag	result	last
pierced	wear	housewife	suicide	unusual
remember		Ireland	winner	wooden
		knife		

1   The identity of a headless _____ found in a woodland near Brighton will not be positively known until dental records have been checked.

2   So Carol, you're a _____ and a mother. Have you got any children?

3   My mum said I used to fight my way out of my cot. But I can't _____ . That was before my time.

4   EARS _____ WHILE YOU WAIT

5   Alligator for sale. Would exchange for a _____ leg.

6   After viewing the headless, legless and armless corpse, Detective Inspector Brown said that he no longer thought this was a case of _____ .

7   He is going for the pink, and for those of you with _____ TV sets, the yellow is behind the blue.

8   Don't tell all those coming in the final _____ of that fantastic match, but let's have another look at Italy's winning goal.

9   I've _____ the lyrics note by note.

10 *Sign outside a carpenter's shop:*
Handyman – can _____ anything. Bell doesn't work. Please shout.

11 If you cannot read, take one of these _____ .

12 *Advert in an African newspaper:*
Old-established manufacturer of suspension bridges _____ door-to-door salesman.

13 You couldn't get me on Mars if it were the _____ place on Earth.

14 Remember, postcards only please. The _____ will be the first one opened.

15 Bachelor (40) non-driver, would accompany same on car tour of _____.

16 'I wish he wouldn't _____ his old sports jacket – it makes him look a freak,' said Mrs O'Sullivan, wife of Brighton ex-officer showman who wears a 3-inch ivory ring in his _____ , 5-inch daggers in his ears and is dyed _____ all over.

17 There will be a procession next Sunday afternoon in the grounds of the Monastery, but if it rains in the afternoon the procession will _____ in the morning.

18 *A small ad in a Nairobi newspaper:* Young farm worker wishes to marry beautiful girl with tractor. Please send _____ of tractor.

19 *Obituary notice:* FLINDERS, Frederick John. Accidentally killed last Saturday when a _____ ricocheted while he was trying to shoot a rabbit in his vegetable garden. Surviving are his wife, three children and one rabbit.

20 *Japanese whisky advert:* World's finest whisky made from Scotland's best _____.

21 To avoid burning your hands with hot water _____ the water first before putting your hands in.

From FUN CLASS ACTIVITIES: Book 1 by Peter Watcyn-Jones © Penguin Books 2000 PHOTOCOPIABLE

39 SILLY SIGNS 1

Fill in the missing words in the signs and notices below. Choose from the following. Not all the words will be used.

verbs		nouns		other words
feed	send	bar	guard	enough
guarantee	suggest	customer	soldier	except
hope	visit	dogs	waitress	however
lost	wait	door		not
regret		garage		other
				unfortunately

1 *Sign in a Bucharest Hotel*

The lift is being fixed for the next day. During that time we _____ that you will be unbearable.

2 *Hospital sign*

GUARD _____
OPERATING

3 *Sign in a Moscow cemetery*

You are welcome to visit the cemetery where famous Russian and Soviet composers, artists and writers are buried daily, _____
Thursdays.

4 *Sign in a Tel Aviv hotel*

If you wish breakfast, lift the telephone, and our _____ will arrive. This will be _____ to bring up your food.

5 *Sign in an Indian restaurant*

AFTER ONE VISIT WE _____ YOU WILL BE REGULAR

6 *Sign at a Hairdresser's*

HAIRCUTS HALF PRICE TODAY. ONLY ONE PER _____

7 *Sign in a Copenhagen airline ticket office*

WE TAKE YOUR BAGS AND _____ THEM IN ALL DIRECTIONS

8 *Sign in a Norwegian hotel cocktail lounge*

LADIES ARE REQUESTED_____ TO HAVE CHILDREN AT THE _____

9 *Sign in a Budapest zoo*

PLEASE DO NOT _____ THE ANIMALS.
If you have any suitable food, give it to the _____ on duty.

10 *Sign in a doctor's surgery in Rome*

SPECIALIST IN WOMEN AND _____ DISEASES

11 *Sign in an Istanbul hotel*

TO CALL ROOM SERVICE, PLEASE OPEN _____ AND CALL ROOM SERVICE

12 *Sign in an Irish hotel*

Please do not lock the door as we have _____ the key.

40 SILLY SIGNS 2

Fill in the missing words in the signs and notices below. Choose from the following. Not all the words will be used.

verbs		**nouns**		**other words**	
bought	singing	absence	feet	exciting	out of order
cancelled	sleeps	complaints	manager	most	rather
pay	sold	death	problem	neatly	upside-down
prosecuted	spoken			on account of	while
said	walking			instant	
should					

1 *Sign in an Indian bookshop*

SPOKEN ENGLISH
_____ HERE

2 *Sign on the grass in a park*

YOUR _____ ARE
KILLING ME!

3 *Sign on the window of a health food shop*

CLOSED _____
SICKNESS

4 *Sign in an estate agent's window*

HONEYMOON luxury flat.
_____ three.

5 *Sign outside a photographer's*

CHILDREN'S HEADS
_____ EXECUTED

6 *Sign at a railway station*

BEWARE! TO TOUCH
THESE WIRES IS
_____ DEATH.
ANYONE FOUND
DOING SO WILL BE
_____

7 *Sign on a Hotel lift*

PLEASE DO NOT USE
LIFT WHEN IT IS

_____

8 *Sign on staff notice board of department store*

IF YOU THINK YOU'VE '
GOT A _____ , YOU
_____ SEE THE
MANAGER.

9 *Sign in a Polish restaurant*

AS FOR THE LUNCH
SERVED YOU AT THE
HOTEL MONOPOL, YOU
WILL BE _____ ITS
PRAISES TO YOUR
GRANDCHILDREN ON
YOUR DEATHBED

10 *Sign in a Beauty parlour*

Ears pierced _____ you
wait. _____ for TWO
and get another ONE
pierced FREE.

11 *Sign in a Mexico City hotel*

BROKEN ENGLISH
_____ PERFECTLY

10 *Sign in a London hotel*

CUSTOMERS SHOULD NOTE THAT ANY _____
ABOUT RUDENESS IN THE STAFF WILL BE DEALT
WITH _____ SEVERELY

41 COURTROOM ENGLISH

Fill in the missing words in the dialogues below. Not all of the words will be used.

verbs		adjectives		nouns	
arrest	identify	acquainted	married	gun	knife
commit	prove	foreign	present	height	partnership
describe	recognise	interested	successful	husband	relationship
hesitated	stood back				

A

Lawyer: Can you (1)_____ the individual?

Witness: He was about medium (2)_____ and had a beard.

Lawyer: Was this a male or a female?

B

Lawyer: I'll show you Exhibit 3 and ask if you (3)_____ that picture.

Witness: That's me.

Lawyer: Were you (4)_____ when that picture was taken?

C

Lawyer: Have you ever tried to (5)_____ suicide?

Witness: Yes, sir.

Lawyer: Were you ever (6)_____?

D

Lawyer: What is your (7)_____ with the plaintiff?

Witness: She is my daughter.

Lawyer: Was she your daughter on February 13th 1992?

E

Lawyer: Were you (8)_____ with the deceased?

Witness: Yes.

Lawyer: Was this before or after she died?

F

Lawyer: Are you (9)_____?

Witness: No, I'm divorced.

Lawyer: And what did your (10)_____ do before you divorced him?

Witness: A lot of things that I didn't know about.

G

Lawyer: What happened then?

Witness: He told me, he says 'I have to kill you because you can (11)_____ me.'

Lawyer: And did he kill you?

H

Lawyer: James (12)_____ and shot Tommy Lee. Is that right?

Witness: Yes.

Lawyer: And then Tommy Lee pulled out his (13)_____ and shot James in the fracas?

Witness: No sir, just above it.

42 EXCUSES, ETC.

Fill in the missing words in the letters below. Choose from the following. Not all the words will be used.

verbs		adjectives		nouns		other words	
changed	refused	absent	late	difference	problem	because of	until
given birth	repeat	annoyed	married	knee	proceedings	ever since	while
insisted	yell	enclosed	unable	pay	psychiatrist	no longer	

Doctors' notes

A The patient has been depressed (1)_____ she began seeing me in 1983.

B He had a left toe amputation one month ago. He also had a left (2)_____ amputation last year.

C The patient is a 79-year-old widow who (3)_____ lives with her husband.

D The patient (4)_____ an autopsy.

Letters to government departments

E In accordance with your instructions I have (5)_____ to twins in the (6)_____ envelope.

F I am very much (7)_____ to find you have branded my son illiterate. This is a dirty lie as I was (8)_____ a week before he was born.

G You have (9)_____ my little boy to a girl. Will this make a (10)_____?

H I cannot get sick (11)_____. I have six children. Can you tell me why?

I Milk is needed for the baby and father is (12)_____ to supply it.

Parents' letters to school

J Please excuse my son being (13)_____ for school yesterday. I forgot to wake him up and did not find him (14)_____ I started making the beds.

K Please excuse Pamela for being (15)_____ yesterday. She had diarrhoea and her boots leak.

Letter to a lawyer

L Please stop the divorce (16)_____ against my wife, Betty. We have stopped fighting and we don't (17)_____ at each other any more. I think we're in love again, but I won't be sure until my (18)_____ tells me.

From FUN CLASS ACTIVITIES: Book 1 by Peter Watcyn-Jones © Penguin Books 2000 PHOTOCOPIABLE

43 EXPAND A TEXT

Working in pairs, try to decide where the following words go in the passage below.

down   either   particularly   rope   so   still   suddenly

Two men were climbing a difficult mountain when one of them fell down a crevasse 500 feet deep.

'Are you all right Bert?' called the man at the top of the crevasse.

'I'm alive, thank goodness, Fred,' came the reply.

'Here, grab this,' said Fred, throwing a rope to Bert.

'I can't grab it,' shouted Bert. 'My arms are broken.'

'Well, fit it round your legs.'

'I'm afraid I can't do that ,' apologised Bert. 'My legs are broken.'

'Put the rope in your mouth,' shouted Fred.

Bert put the rope in his mouth and Fred began to haul him to safety: 490 feet ... 400 feet ... 300 feet ... 200 feet ... 100 feet ... 50 feet ... and then Fred called: 'Are you all right, Bert?'

'Yeh-h-h ... h ... h ... '

44 SHORTEN A TEXT 1

Working in pairs, try to find five words which can be crossed out without the joke losing its meaning.

An Englishman, an Irishman and a tall Scotsman were hiding from armed bandits up palm trees. The bandit chief called up one tree, 'Who's there?' And the Englishman went 'Cheep! Cheep!' loudly, like a bird. So the bandit chief called up the next tree, 'Who's there?' And the Scotsman went 'Eeek! Eeek!' just like a monkey. So the bandit chief called up the next tree, 'Who's there?' And the Irishman went, 'Moo–oo!'

45 SHORTEN A TEXT 2

Working in pairs, try to find five words which can be crossed out without the joke losing its meaning.

On the street stood a middle-aged man, a dog and a black horse. The dog was playing an accordion while the horse sang beautifully, and the man was collecting money from passers-by. One old lady stopped and remarked on what an amazing sight the three made.

'And how very talented you are. You should be performing in a circus.'

'Oh no, madam,' said the man seriously, 'my conscience wouldn't let me do that. I'll let you into a secret, though. The horse can't really sing. The dog's a ventriloquist, actually!'

46 ONE WORD ONLY

Read the joke below and think of the word which best fits each space. Use only one word in each space. Write your answers below. There is an example at the beginning (0).

The school reunion dinner

It was ten years (0)_____ William and Derek had (1)_____ school and in those ten years they had (2)_____ met.

Then, at the school reunion dinner, they sat (3)_____ to each other.

'(4)_____ has life treated you since leaving school?' asked Derek.

'Oh, I've had my (5)_____ and downs. But now I'm doing quite well (6)_____ an estate agent. We've got offices in fifteen towns and villages in the area and hope to open a London (7)_____ next year.'

'That (8)_____ good,' replied Derek.

'And how have you (9)_____ since leaving school?' asked William.

'Not so good,' said Derek. 'You know when I was at school I fancied Fiona? Well, I (10)_____ her soon after school – but (11)_____ three months of marriage she left me. Then my second wife died (12)_____ cancer. The new house I bought by the sea was a bit (13)_____ near it – within a year after (14)_____ it, the cliff it was on fell (15)_____ the sea, taking the house and all my possessions with it. And you probably noticed that I (16)_____ with a limp. That's the result of falling out of my canoe and being crushed (17)_____ a weir. And today didn't start too well, (18)_____ My dog was (19)_____ over and killed by a bus and my motorbike was set on (20)_____ by vandals.'

'But, if you don't (21)_____ me asking,' said William, 'What do you do for a (22)_____?'

'Oh!' replied Derek. 'I sell good (23)_____ charms!'

Write your answers here:

0 since	6 _____	12 _____	18 _____
1 _____	7 _____	13 _____	19 _____
2 _____	8 _____	14 _____	20 _____
3 _____	9 _____	15 _____	21 _____
4 _____	10 _____	16 _____	22 _____
5 _____	11 _____	17 _____	23 _____

47 CHOOSE THE ANSWER 1

Read the joke below and decide which word or words (a, b, c or d) best fits each space. There is an example at the beginning (0).

Meeting an old friend again

A man went to visit a (0)_____ couple who he had not seen (1)_____ more than ten years. The wife opened the (2)_____.

'Hello, Brian. how nice to see you again!' she said.

'It's nice to see you (3)_____, Jean,' said the man. 'And how is (4)_____ husband, David?'

'Oh, (5)_____ you know?' she said. 'David died just over a year (6)_____.'

'Oh, I'm so (7)_____,' said the man. 'Was it sudden?'

'Yes, it (8)_____. One Sunday morning he went into the garden to get a (9)_____ for lunch and dropped (10)_____ dead.'

'(11)_____ awful!' said the man. 'Whatever (12)_____?'

'What could I do?' answered the woman. 'I opened a (13)_____ of peas.'

0	a	old	b	wedding	c	married	d	friend
1	a	since	b	from	c	for	d	at
2	a	door	b	window	c	floor	d	umbrella
3	a	thanks	b	too	c	either	d	well
4	a	it	b	the	c	her	d	your
5	a	can't	b	doesn't	c	don't	d	isn't
6	a	ago	b	since	c	away	d	past
7	a	unhappy	b	glad	c	sorry	d	hungry
8	a	is	b	was	c	did	d	sudden
9	a	cabbage	b	newspaper	c	milk	d	shirt
10	a	away	b	down	c	off	d	out
11	a	That	b	What	c	It	d	How
12	a	did you	b	do you do	c	happened	d	did you do
13	a	parcel	b	tin	c	bottle	d	bunch

48 CHOOSE THE ANSWER 2

Read the joke below and decide which word (a, b, c or d) best fits each space. There is an example at the beginning (0).

The vacuum cleaner salesman

The little old lady was (0)_____ dusting her cottage deep in the countryside when (1)_____ was a knock at the door.

'Good morning, madam,' said a well-dressed young man when she opened the door. 'What a lovely house you've got,' he said, (2)_____ his way into the house. 'I've got something to (3)_____ you that I'm sure you'll be really interested (4)_____.'

'But ...' started the old woman, before being (5)_____ by the young man who had now pulled a large bag of soot, dust and other small (6)_____ of rubbish from his pocket and was (7))_____ them all over her carpet.

'Don't worry,' said the young man. 'What I have in my car outside will soon (8)_____ all this rubbish, dust and soot, and I'll even clean your other rooms too. In fact my new machine is so (9)_____ that it will even suck out ground-in dust and dirt (10)_____ this.' As he spoke, he used his (11)_____ to press the soot and dust into the carpet.

'But ...' tried the old lady again, but without (12)_____ success as the young man had quickly gone out of the front door.

A few minutes (13)_____ he reappeared with a very modern-looking vacuum cleaner.

'Now, where can I (14)_____ this in?' he asked.

'Probably the next village, about ten miles away,' replied the old lady. 'The electricity (15)_____ hasn't (16)_____ here yet.'

0	a	hardly	b	busy	c	active	d	trying
1	a	it	b	came	c	there	d	suddenly
2	a	pushing	b	getting	c	putting	d	placing
3	a	demonstrate	b	show	c	try out	d	present
4	a	of	b	with	c	for	d	in
5	a	persuaded	b	interrupted	c	butted	d	influenced
6	a	ingredients	b	topics	c	containers	d	items
7	a	sprinkling	b	spraying	c	gathering	d	distributing
8	a	take off	b	put away	c	remove	d	destroy
9	a	expensive	b	effective	c	strong	d	organized
10	a	as	b	such	c	like	d	similar
11	a	heel	b	shoulder	c	ankle	d	thigh
12	a	some	b	much	c	none	d	little
13	a	later	b	ago	c	after	d	following
14	a	connect	b	join	c	insert	d	plug
15	a	companies	b	wires	c	power	d	supply
16	a	arrived	b	appeared	c	reached	d	started

49 FILL IN THE VERBS 1

In the following true crime stories a number of verbs have been left out. Try to put them back in again. Choose from the verbs in brackets after each paragraph and put them in the correct tense. Not all the verbs will be used.

A

Rolf Horne, a 40-year-old Norwegian bank robber, (1)_____ with £3,000 in February 1993, but the police (2)_____ him two hours later when he (3)_____ to (4)_____ an account at the same bank in Oslo, Norway.

(arrest, escape, follow, invest, open, run away, try)

Wilhelmina Elden, a teller at the bank, said, 'I couldn't (5)_____ my eyes when the same guy (6)_____ into the bank again and asked to (7)_____ the money he (8)_____ that morning.' He (9)_____ police later that he (10)_____ afraid of being robbed and (11)_____ to (12)_____ it somewhere safe.

(be, believe, borrow, deposit, get, put, steal, tell, understand, walk, want)

B

Labourer Maphupu Molatudi, aged 55, (13)_____ asleep in a hostel north of Johannesburg, South Africa, in February 1996, when a robber (14)_____ to (15)_____ open his mouth and (16)_____ his false teeth.

(be, force, give up, have, steal, stop, try, want)

Not surprisingly, Molatudi (17)_____, but the thief (18)_____ him with his fists, (19)_____ him by the throat and (20)_____ his teeth anyway. The police later (21)_____ a suspect , but Molatudi never (22)_____ his teeth back.

(arrest, be, beat, eat, get, grab, take, tickle, wake up)

50 FILL IN THE VERBS 2

In the following true crime stories a number of verbs have been left out. Try to put them back in again. Choose from the verbs in brackets after each paragraph and put them in the correct tense. Not all the verbs will be used.

A

A few years ago, Indonesian police (1)_____ a man in Jakarta for (2)_____ 'magic pencils' at £225 each, which he (3)_____ would automatically (4)_____ correct answers to university entrance exams.

(arrest, catch, claim, produce, sell, suggest, understand)

They (5)_____ about £2,600 from sales of the pencils, which (6)_____ on sale for almost a whole year. The man (7)_____ the police that the pencils were equipped with copper wire and electronic signals which would (8)_____ the computers that were used for (9)_____ the exams and would (10)_____ wrong answers. Dozens of students (11)_____ when the magic didn't (12)_____ for them.

(appear, be, complain, confiscate, confuse, correct, get, mark, take, tell, work)

B

When Patricia Wakelin of Westbury-on-Trym (13)_____ her Ford Fiesta car for sale, David Brice, 28, (14)_____ like the perfect buyer. He (15)_____ with his grandmother and (16)_____ the old lady with Mrs Wakelin while he (17)_____ the car for a test drive.

(advertise, depart, leave, seem, sell, steal, take, turn up)

Unfortunately, that was the last she (18)_____ of both him and her car. The old lady (19)_____ not to be his granny at all, but someone who (20)_____ in an old people's home in Bedminster and whom Wakelin (21_____ to take for a drive. In the end, Brice (22)_____ to two years in prison for the car theft and a number of other con tricks he (23)_____ to.

(confess, end up, live, offer, rent, see, send, sentence, turn out)

---

51 FILL IN THE VERBS 3

In the following true story a number of verbs have been left out. Try to put them back in again. Choose from the verbs in brackets after each paragraph and put them in the correct tense. Not all the verbs will be used.

Professor Marvo, a magician in Argentina, (1)_____ to a sticky end when one of his tricks was just too believable for his own good. (2)_____ to a small crowd in a tavern in Azul, he (3)_____ his act by (4)_____ a bullet, fired by his assistant, in his teeth. In reality, the assistant (5)_____ a blank and the magician simply (6)_____ a bullet he (7)_____ in his mouth.

(act, catch, come, disguise, finish off, fire, get, hide, perform, produce)

But Marco Asprella, a 48-year-old gold miner in the audience, (8)_____ this. He was so impressed by the trick that he (9)_____ his own 45-calibre handgun and, (10)_____ 'Catch this one, Professor!', (11)_____ it straight into Marco's face, almost (12)_____ his head off.

(blow, fire, forget, miss, put off, take out, throw, yell)

He was stunned that he (13)_____ the magician and all through his trial (14)_____ it clear that he didn't (15)_____ why the man hadn't (16)_____ his bullet. The jury (17)_____ and (18)_____ him of the charge of murder.

However, he (19)_____ guilty of (20)_____ a concealed weapon, for which he (21)_____ a small fine and was also (22)_____ on probation for two years.

(acquit, carry, catch, find, force, hide, kill, make,
put, receive, release, sympathise, understand)

52 FIND THE MISTAKES

Read the joke below and look carefully at each line. Some of the lines are correct, and some have a word which should not be there. If a line is correct, put a tick (✔) after it. If a line has a word which should not be there, write down that word. There are two examples at the beginning (0) and (00).

The Great Escape

0	An Englishman, a Welshman and a Scotsman	✔
00	who had been caught smuggling drugs and had	who
1	been sentenced to the death by firing squad in a	
2	remote South American capital. First the	
3	Englishman was taken out of his cell and put up	
4	against the wall. As the soldiers raised up their	
5	rifles, and the captain said, 'Ready … Aim …' the	
6	Englishman shouted at the top of his voice,	
7	'Avalanche!'	
8	The soldiers dropped their rifles in a panic and	
9	ran away. In the confusion, the Englishman was	
10	managed to escape.	
11	When the Scotsman's turn came to be shot, he	
12	decided to follow after his friend's example. He	
13	shouted 'Flood!' at the crucial moment and had made	
14	his escape in the same fashion.	
15	Last came the Welshman. He had watched the	
16	others and felt himself confident that he could	
17	escape away in the same manner. The soldiers	
18	raised their rifles, the captain said once again to	
19	'Ready … Aim …' as the Welshman shouted at the	
20	top of his voice, 'Fire!'	

53 CAN YOU READ IT?

In the following text there are letters missing from various words. See how well you can read the text, adding the missing letters.

Letter from a loving mother

Dear son,

Just a few lines to let you know I'm still alive. I'm writ– – – this let– – –
slowly bec– – – – I kn– – you can't re – – fast. Y– – won't kn– – the ho– – –
when y– – get h– – – because we ha– – moved.

Ab– – – your fath– –. He h– – a lov– – – new j– –. He h– – five hun– – – – men
und– – him. He cu– – grass at the cemet– – –. Th– – – was a wash– – –
machine in t– – new ho– – – when we mov– – in b– – it hasn't be– – working
t– – well. La– – week I p– – Dad's sh– – – in, pul– – – the cha– – and haven't
se– – it sin– –.

Your sis– – –, Mary, h– – a ba– – this morn– – – but I hav– –'– found o– – if
it's a b– – or a gi– – yet, so I do–'– know if y– – are an au– – or an un– – –.

I we– – to the doc– – – last Thur– – – – and yo– – father ca– – with me. T– –
doctor p– – a sm– – – glass tu– – in my mou– – and to– – me n– – to ta – –
for ten min– – – –. Your fath– – offered to b– – it o– – him.

It on– – rained tw– – – this we– –, first f– – three da– – and th– – for fo– –.

We h– – a let– – – from t– – undertaker. He sa– – if t– – last paym– – – on
yo – – grandfather's pl– – isn't pa– – within sev– – days, th– – up he co– – –.

Your lov– – – mother.

P.S.
I was going to send you £10 but I had already sealed up the envelope.

From FUN CLASS ACTIVITIES: Book 1 by Peter Watcyn-Jones © Penguin Books 2000 PHOTOCOPIABLE

54 SORT OUT THE MISSING WORDS

Read through the following joke and then choose the best phrase given below to fill each of the gaps. Write one letter (a–r). Not all the phrases will be used.

Survival in the desert

An Englishman, a Welshman and a Scotsman are travelling in the desert (1)_____ some ten miles from the nearest village. There is nothing for it (2)_____, under the cruel, pitiless sun, (3)_____. The Englishman takes an umbrella, the Scotsman a water-bottle (4)_____ the door of the jeep and carries it with him.

But (5)_____ when, quite unexpectedly, salvation appeared (6)_____. The leader of the caravan agreed to assist them to the village. He (7)_____ and a camel each to ride upon.

'But tell me,' he said to the Englishman. 'Why (8)_____ an umbrella in the desert? There (9)_____ for many years.'

'It isn't to protect me from the rain,' replied the Englishman, 'but (10)_____.'

'Ah!' says the leader of the caravan. 'Truly the Englishman is wise. And you, my friend,' he said to the Scotsman, 'why do you carry this bottle?'

'I decided,' said the Scotsman, 'that thirst would be the greatest problem (11)_____ ten miles across the hot sand, so I emptied out the water (12)_____!'

'Ah!' said the leader of the caravan. 'Truly the Scotsman is wise. And you, my friend,' (13)_____, 'why do you carry the door of your vehicle?'

'I (14)_____,' said the Welshman, 'so I thought if I carried the door and it got too hot I could always (15)_____.'

a	and filled it with good Scotch whisky	k	in the shape of a camel caravan
b	and the Welshman rips off	l	inside the leader's tent
c	but to walk across the burning sand	m	they had only walked two or three miles
d	do you carry	n	to protect me from the sun
e	gave them food and drink	o	unless they get help soon
f	has not been rain in these parts	p	when it starts raining
g	he said to the Welshman	q	when their jeep breaks down
h	was worried about the heat	r	wind down the window
i	if they are not to die of thirst		
j	if we had to walk		

From FUN CLASS ACTIVITIES: Book 1 by Peter Watcyn-Jones © Penguin Books 2000 PHOTOCOPIABLE

55 WHAT'S MISSING?

Read the joke below and look carefully at each line. Some of the lines are correct, and some have a word missing. If a line is correct, put a tick (✔) after it. If a line has a missing word, use a stroke (/) to show where the word has been left out and suggest what the missing word might be. There are two examples at the beginning (0) and (00).

Looking for a hotel room

0	I once went for / short holiday to Brighton.	a
00	Unfortunately, a political conference was going	✔
1	on and I couldn't find anywhere to stay.	
2	I wandered about, up down the promenade,	
3	went to every hotel but I still couldn't find	
4	anywhere to rest my head. Then eventually I	
5	wandered the road towards the sea, and I	
6	heard a voice which crying in distress.	
7	'Help! Help! I'm drowning!'	
8	I bravely to the edge of the water and said,	
9	'What's that? What you say?'	
10	And the voice repeated, 'Help! I'm drowning!'	
11	I said, 'You tell me your name, please?'	
12	She said, 'I'm Miss Brown. Help! I'm drowning!'	
13	I said, 'Are you staying, Miss Brown?'	
14	She said, 'I'm staying at the Bay View Hotel ...'	
15	That was the last thing she ever said.	
16	So I went straight off the Bay View Hotel, walked	
17	straight up to the reception desk and to the	
18	receptionist, 'Have you got a Miss Brown	
19	staying?'	
20	'Yes, ' she replied. 'In Room 201.'	
21	I said, 'I'm afraid she's fallen into the sea and	
22	drowned. Could I her room, please?'	
23	Just the owner appeared in the doorway.	
24	'Sorry,' she said, 'I've just given it to the gentleman	
25	pushed her in!'	

From FUN CLASS ACTIVITIES: Book 1 by Peter Watcyn-Jones © Penguin Books 2000 PHOTOCOPIABLE

56 BOOKING A ROOM AT A HOTEL (DIALOGUE)

Act out the part of B acccording to what it says on your card.

(A=receptionist B=member of the public)

At the reception desk of a hotel.

A: Good afternoon. Can I help you?

B: Yes, I'd like a room, please.

A: A single room?

B: Yes, just for tonight. With a bath.

A: Single room with bath ... just a minute, please. *(slight pause)*

   I'm sorry, we've only got double rooms left for tonight.

B: Are you sure?

A: Yes, quite sure. This is a very busy time for us.

B: How much is a double room?

A: £90, including breakfast.

B: No, that's too much.

A: I'm sorry, but that's all we've got.

B: Ah well, I suppose I'll have to try somewhere else. Goodbye.

A: Goodbye.

You are angry and in a bad mood.
You are feeling romantic and flirtatious.
You are very shy and find it hard to look people in the face when you speak to them.
You are slightly deaf and tend to speak too loudly.
You are very nervous and your voice is shaking.
You are dying to go to the toilet.
You are very upset and feel tearful because you have just had some bad news.
You are having problems speaking because you've just been to the dentist.
You are very friendly and cheerful and smile a lot.
You are a 'foreigner' and are not very good at English.
You are very tired and can hardly keep awake.
You are a bit short-sighted and like to get really close to people when you talk to them.
You have a slight stutter, especially when you try to say words that start with 's' or 'p'.
You have a problem with your right eye and keep 'winking' all the time.
You are an opera singer and tend to 'sing' your words.
You have a terrible cold and keep sneezing and having to blow your nose.

57 EXPLAIN YOURSELF!

You were sitting on your neighbour's roof at 11.30 last night.
You were fighting with a policeman outside the cinema last Saturday.
You were at a restaurant with a very beautiful woman/handsome man.
You were running through the park dressed as Superman and shouting 'Wait for me!'
You and your friends were throwing stones at a bus.
You were sitting at the top of a tree in your garden at 1 o'clock in the morning singing 'Happy birthday to you!'
You were climbing through your neighbour's window in your pyjamas at midnight.
You were walking through the park with a baby gorilla.
You were lying in front of a bus outside your house. (You had not been run over!)
You took your sister's baby out for a walk in his pram and came back with a different baby and pram.

Dialogue 1

At a party.

A: Excuse me.
B: Yes?
A: Do you mind if I join you?
B: No, not at all.
A: Thank you. I just wanted to talk to someone before I killed myself.

Dialogue 2

In a park.

A: Is that your child over there?
B: Yes. Why do you ask?
A: Because he just bit my dog!

Dialogue 3

On a train.

A: Tickets, please.
B: Sorry?
A: Your ticket please, sir/madam.
B: My ticket? Don't you know who I am?
A: Sorry, I'm afraid I don't. But whoever you are, could I just see your ticket, please?
B: But I'm Zzroomp from the planet Zorca!

Dialogue 4

At home. There is a knock at the door. You answer it.

A: Yes?
B: Help! Please help me!
A: What do you mean?
B: Please help me! I'm turning into a frog!

Dialogue 5

At home. The phone rings.

A: …(say your name and telephone number)
B: Hello. This is…(say your name)
A: Oh, hello…(repeat person's name). Look, if it's about last night…
B: YOU BET IT'S ABOUT LAST NIGHT!!

Dialogue 6

At home. The phone rings.

A: …(say your telephone number) (Say your name), speaking.
B: I'm phoning about your advertisement in today's newspaper.
A: Oh, about the pet crocodile?
B: Yes, that's right.

59 CONSEQUENCES

Don't forget to fold your sheet so that what you have written is hidden before passing it on to someone else.

_____

(Write down the name of a man everyone in the class will know.)

FOLD

met

(Write down the name of a woman everyone in the class will know.)

FOLD

in/at/on

(Write down where they met.)

FOLD

He was wearing

FOLD

And she was wearing

FOLD

He said to her:

FOLD

And she replied:

FOLD

Then they decided to

FOLD

As a result they

FOLD

Now they are both looking forward to

_____

Work in Groups A and B. You are A.

The crossword below is only half filled in. Group B also have a crossword that is only half filled in. Take it in turns to ask what the missing words are (e.g. 'What's 4 Across?') and answer by trying to **mime** each word. When miming, you are allowed to make noises, but you are not allowed to use any words.

Here are the words you will have to mime for Group B. Before you start, make sure you understand them.

ballet	deaf	hungry	tent
clown	elephant	kiss	toilet
cry	fat	love	typewriter
dance	freezing	musician	unhappy

Work in Groups A and B. You are B.

The crossword below is only half filled in. Group A also have a crossword that is only half filled in. Take it in turns to ask what the missing words are (e.g. 'What's 1 Down?') and answer by trying to **mime** each word. When miming, you are allowed to make noises, but you are not allowed to use any words.

Here are the words you will have to mime for Group A. Before you start, make sure you understand them.

afraid	doctor	pilot	teacher
angry	dog	shower	throw
baby	heavy	swim	toothache
cycle	pig	yawn	umbrella

61 TONGUE TWISTERS

Six slim slender saplings.	Which switch is the switch for Ipswich?
Ted threw Fred three free throws.	Which wristwatches are Swiss wristwatches.
Pink silk socks with seven silk spots.	The fish and chip shop's chips are soft chips.
Thirty free flowers for three lucky thieves.	She says she shall never sew a sheet.
They threw three thick things.	We surely shall see the sun shine soon.
Red leather, yellow leather.	Can Kitty cuddle Clara's kitten?
Two tubby teddy bears toasting thirty-three tasty tea-cakes.	On the beach I saw six small seals.
The sun shines on shop signs.	There's no need to light a night-light on a night like tonight.
The rat ran by the river with a lump of raw liver	Three grey geese in the green, green grass.
Charlie Saunders chose cheese, cherries and sherry.	Peter Piper picked up a piece of paper.

62 TEST YOUR LOGIC

Work in pairs Try to work out the answers to the following problems.

1 Why can't a person living in London be buried in Scotland?

_____

2 Some months have 30 days and some have 31. How many months have 28 days?

_____

3 How many children does a man have if he has ten sons and each son has a sister?

_____

4 An Air France Boeing 747 crashes on the border between France and Belgium. On board are 150 French people and 200 Belgians. Where are the survivors buried – in France or in Belgium?

_____

5 I am a woman. If Sally's daughter is my daughter's mother, what relationship am I to Sally?

(a) her grandmother (b) her mother
(c) her daughter (d) her aunt

_____

6 What was the highest mountain on Earth before Mount Everest was discovered?

_____

7 If you had only one match and entered a dark room containing an oil lamp, a newspaper, and some kindling wood, what would you light first?

_____

8 A farmer had 17 sheep. All but 9 died. How many did he have left?

_____

9 Write this down as one number: 15 thousand, 15 hundred and 15.

_____

10 Mrs Taylor's bungalow is decorated entirely in pink. Her lamps, walls, carpets and ceilings are all pink. What colour are her stairs?

_____

11 Take three apples from five apples. How many do you have?

_____

12 If Mr Wright's peacock laid an egg in Mr Blake's garden, who is the rightful owner of the egg?

_____

13 What do you sit on, sleep on, and brush your teeth with?

_____

14 How many times can you take 4 from 33?

_____

15 A man left his hotel and walked towards the car park. Without the benefit of moonlight or any artificial light, he was able to spot his black car 100 metres away. How was this possible?

_____

16 Which is correct: 'Nine and seven is fifteen' or 'Nine and seven are fifteen?'

_____

17 If a woman was born in Italy, raised in Australia, married a Scotsman, lived in England then died in Italy, what is she?

_____

TOTAL SCORE:

_____

From FUN CLASS ACTIVITIES: Book 1 by Peter Watcyn-Jones © Penguin Books 2000 PHOTOCOPIABLE

63 COMPLETE THE CROSSWORD

Twenty-five words are missing from the three jokes below. Complete the following crossword by working out what these missing words are.

(Down ↓ , Across →)

Joke 1

Two elephants _____(20 Down) to a fair.
'Let's have a ride on the merry-go-round!'
_____(4 Down) the first.
'_____(1 Down) make me giddy!' said the
second. 'You go _____(3 Across) I'll watch.'
So the first elephant agreed. But after a
_____(5 Down) or two the merry-go-round
went out of control. It spun faster and faster,
_____(2 Down) the elephant was thrown off.
'Are you hurt?' cried the _____(16 Across)
elephant, hurrying up.
'Of _____(17 Down) I am!' replied the first
elephant, rather shaken. 'I went round five
_____(7 Down) and you didn't even wave!'

Joke 2

_____(10 Down) was once a baby _____(20
Across) was very quiet. He never said 'Mama' or
'Dada'. He never said _____(6 Across). When
he was three he _____(21 Across) hadn't said
anything, and his mum and dad were worried.
_____(13 Down) he was five he still hadn't

said anything and they were _____(5 Across)
worried than ever.
Then one day when he was _____(22 Across)
his dinner, he said, 'Not enough salt!'
'Goodness me,' said his mum. 'You can
_____(19 Down)! Why is it all these years
you've never said anything?'
'Well,' said the boy, 'up until now _____(11
Across) has been all right.'

Joke 3

Mr and Mrs Brown were going on their first
_____(9 Down) abroad and Mrs Brown had
spent a long _____(19 Across) fussing over
what they _____(8 Across) take with them.
At last they _____(18 Across) at the airport.
'I do wish I'd _____(15 Down) the television,'
sighed Mrs Brown.
'Whatever for?' _____(14 Down) her
husband.
'I _____(12 Across) the tickets on it,'
she replied.

From FUN CLASS ACTIVITIES: Book 1 by Peter Watcyn-Jones © Penguin Books 2000 PHOTOCOPIABLE

Knock, knock. Who's there? Roland. Roland who? Roland butter, please!	Knock, knock. Who's there? Tish. Tish who? Bless you! Have you caught a cold?	Knock, knock. Who's there? Howard. Howard who? Howard you like to know.
Knock, knock. Who's there? Juno. Juno who? Juno what time it is?	Knock, knock. Who's there? Water. Water who? Water you staring at?	Knock, knock. Who's there? Andy. Andy who? And he bit me again.
Knock, knock. Who's there? Boo. Boo who? There's no need to cry. It's only a joke.	Knock, knock. Who's there? Andrew. Andrew who? Andrew a lovely picture of me.	Knock, knock. Who's there? Egburt. Egburt who? Egg but no bacon.
Knock, knock. Who's there? Aida. Aida who? Aida sandwich at break time.	Knock, knock. Who's there? Wanda. Wanda who? Wanda what the time is.	Knock knock, Who's there? Bean. Bean who? Bean working hard lately.
Knock knock, Who's there? Ice cream. Ice cream who? Ice cream and scream and scream until I'm sick.	Knock knock, Who's there? Andy. Andy who? Andy bit me on the finger!	Knock knock, Who's there? Owen. Owen who? Owen are you going to let me come in?
Knock knock, Who's there? N. E. N. E. who? N. E. body you like, so long as you let me in.	Knock knock, Who's there? Tuba. Tuba who? Tuba toothpaste, please.	Knock knock, Who's there? Wood. Wood who? Wood you believe it – I've forgotten.
Knock, knock. Who's there? Gladys. Gladys who? Gladys Friday.	Knock, knock. Who's there? Ida. Ida who? Ida terrible time getting here.	Knock, knock. Who's there? Sonia. Sonia who? Sonia foot. I can smell it from here.
Knock, knock. Who's there? Amos. Amos who? A mosquito just bit me.	Knock knock. Who's there? Owl. Owl who? Owl you know unless you open the door?	Knock, knock. Who's there? Jester. Jester who? Jester song at twilight.

Customer: Do you have rice pudding on the menu?	**Customer:** Waiter! I can't eat this food. Fetch the manager.	**Customer:** Waiter! This milk is very watery.
Customer: Waiter, why is there a button on my plate?	**Customer:** Waiter, there's a fly in my soup.	**Customer:** Waiter, you've got your thumb in my soup.
Customer: Excuse me, will my hamburger be long?	**Customer:** Waiter! My boiled egg is bad.	**Customer:** Waiter! Does this restaurant have any clean tablecloths?
Customer: Do you serve women in this bar?	**Customer:** Waiter, what's this fly doing in my soup?	**Customer:** Do you serve crabs here?
Customer: Waiter, why is this piece of toast all broken?	**Customer:** *(Looking at steak on his plate)* Waiter, didn't you hear me say 'Well done?'	**Customer:** Waiter, there's soap in this pie.

Waiter: We did, but I wiped it off.	**Waiter:** It's no use, sir, he won't eat it either.	**Waiter:** The cow must have been out in the rain, sir.
Waiter: I expect it's off the jacket potato, sir.	**Waiter:** Don't worry, sir. That spider on your bread will get him.	**Waiter:** That's all right, sir. It's not hot.
Waiter: No, sir, it'll be round.	**Waiter:** Nothing I can do about it, sir. I only laid the table.	**Waiter:** I'm sorry, sir. But I've only been here for six months.
Waiter: No, sir, you must bring your own.	**Waiter:** It looks like the backstroke, sir.	**Waiter:** We serve anyone, sir.
Waiter: Well you said, 'Toast, coffee, and step on it.'	**Waiter:** Yes, sir. And I'd like to thank you for your compliment. We don't get many around here.	**Waiter:** That's to wash it down with, sir.

From FUN CLASS ACTIVITIES: Book 1 by Peter Watcyn-Jones © Penguin Books 2000 *PHOTOCOPIABLE*